.95

D0014739

~tholicism

TRUTH *vs.* DOGMA

TRUTH
vs.
DOGMA

by
J. C. MACAULAY
Pastor, Wheaton Bible Church

Author, *The Word Made Flesh,*
Obedient Unto Death

5793

MOODY PRESS
153 Institute Place
Chicago, Illinois

Printed in the United States of America

PREFACE

The chapters of this book were given first of all as messages in the Wheaton Bible Church. The studies aroused keen interest and elicited many earnest inquiries, particularly from college students. This unexpected response suggested that the chapters might be profitable to others if put in permanent form

I wish to have it clearly understood that I harbor no animosity toward Roman Catholics, and I would gladly champion their right to religious freedom if it were jeopardized. I have been more and more profoundly convinced, however, that Protestants in general are quite ignorant of the teachings of Roman Catholicism. My first thought, therefore, in preaching these sermons, and now in publishing them, was to instruct our Protestant Christians in the true differences between the two faiths. I have been pleased to learn, however, of profit to Roman Catholics through the reading of some of these chapters in manuscript form, and I trust that the volume now sent forth may accomplish this double purpose of instructing those of my own faith, and turning some who have been taught in the sacramentarianism of Rome to the freedom of the gospel of our Lord Jesus Christ.

I have given my utmost endeavor to be entirely fair to the Roman position, and I believe I have presented their point of view accurately. I now commit the work to our Lord for its further ministry, praying that He may be glorified, His people blessed, and many brought to a saving knowledge of our Lord and Saviour Jesus Christ.

J. C. M.

Wheaton, Illinois

5

CONTENTS

Chapter One

ROMAN INFALLIBLES

"To the law and to the testimony: if they speak not according to this word, it is because there is no light in them" *Isaiah* 8:20.

MATTHEW tells us how the scribes and the Pharisees found fault with the disciples of Jesus for not washing their hands before meals, the ground of their complaint being religious, not hygienic. "Why do thy disciples transgress the tradition of the elders?" Our Lord's reply was as stinging as it was startling: "Why do ye also transgress the commandment of God by your tradition?" He backed up his charge by referring to their dogma of corban, by which these hypocrites released themselves from their plain duty under the fifth commandment, then applied to them the scorching words of the prophet: "But in vain they do worship me, teaching for doctrines the commandments of men" (Matt. 15:9).

The Roman church is the perfect successor of the scribes and Pharisees in respect of this substitution of traditions and commandments of men for the plain teaching of Holy Scripture. Secondary authorities have been introduced, and become primary, while the primary authority of God's Word has been relegated to secondary place. Because this question of authority is basic to any comparison of the teachings of Rome with our evangelical position, we must begin here.

This extension of authority beyond the range of Holy Scripture is carried in several directions. First, the apocryphal books are given canonicity, introducing a corrupt element into the Sacred Volume; next, the apostolical and ecclesiastical traditions are added as "the unwritten word," and made binding upon all consciences; then, the church's interpretations claim the full authority and sanction of original revelation. Apocrypha, tradition, interpretation—these are the things added, with which the Holy Scriptures are made to share their glory of divine authority and infallibility.

The apocryphal books need not detain us. With all their interest to the biblical scholar, they utterly lack the stamp of divine inspiration so patent in the true canonical works, which, by their unity, spiritual force, and self-authenticating power, have consistently held their place as "the Word of God."

The traditions profess to give information, not included in the Scriptures, concerning the beginnings of our Christian faith. If the text of Scripture has required very special care to preserve it from corruption through the centuries, it certainly would require continuous miracle to keep tradition from degenerating into trash. Now it was exactly to avoid this that our Scriptures were given us. Luke specifically states the purpose of his writing—"That thou mightest know the certainty of these things, wherein thou hast been instructed." Memory and repetition were not to be trusted with so sacred and vital a deposit. The truth of Scripture is demonstrable, but tradition defies investigation; its only props are the dogma of infallibility, and the authority of the church. The Council of Trent, at its fourth session (1546), decreed "that all should receive with equal reverence the books of the Old and New Testaments, and the traditions concerning faith and manners, as proceeding from the mouth of Christ, or inspired by the Holy Spirit, and preserved in the Catholic Church; and that whosoever knowingly, or of deliberate purpose, despised traditions, should be anathema."

If this equality with the Holy Scriptures is to be firmly secured for the traditions, the council which decrees it so must bear authority enough to make it so. Thus the council, that is, the church, is vested with absolute authority in matters of faith and practice, and its decrees are regarded as indisputable, carrying all the finality of divine law. The church becomes the infallible guide, the sole interpreter, and the "faithful" must not exercise their own hermeneutical powers, but receive the Word as interpreted by the church without question.

This prerogative of the church is centered in the supreme pontiff, the Bishop of Rome, the Pope, who is regarded as the Vicar of Christ on earth, successor to Peter. Actually the dogma of papal infallibility was not laid down as such till the Vatican Council of 1870, but that was only the enunciation of what had long been claimed and acted upon. In keeping with this, Pope Pius IV confirmed the decrees of the Council of Trent in a bull issued in 1564. The pope is regarded as the supreme and infallible interpreter of the Christian faith.

We ought to understand this doctrine of papal infallibility in fairness to ourselves as well as to our Catholic friends. Let one of them define it. I quote Dr. John A. O'Brien, one of the most popular apologists of the Roman church today:

What, then, does infallibility really mean? Simply this: When the Pope in his official capacity, with the fullness of his authority, as successor of St. Peter and head of the Church on earth, proclaims a doctrine on faith or morals binding on the whole Church, he is preserved from error. It is to be noted that three conditions are required: (1) The

Pope must speak *ex cathedra,* i.e., from the Chair of Peter, in his official capacity; (2) the decision must be binding on the whole Church; (3) it must be on a matter of faith or morals.

The Pope has no authority to invent a new doctrine. He is not the author of revelation, but only its interpreter and expounder.[1]

Papal infallibility is a prerogative exercised in the interpretive functions alone, according to the statement of the Vatican Council: "The Holy Spirit was not promised to the successors of Peter in order that they might spread abroad new doctrine which He reveals, but that, under His assistance, they might guard inviolably, and with fidelity explain, the revelation or deposit of faith handed down by the apostles." But certainly the church, by papal authority, holds doctrines and demands practices that the most vivid imagination could not discover in Scripture nor the most specious reasoning adduce from it. Where do these come from? Tradition. Papal infallibility is thus utilized to bolster tradition, till the most amazing and pretentious claims are concreted into dogma and set up as binding.

So while we Protestants have our authoritative revelation in the Holy Scriptures, Rome has its additions, its traditions, and its interpretations, all alike binding and equally authoritative with the Bible itself. I do not think any informed Catholic would dispute that statement of the case.

Such a situation demands examination. First, it is the way of heresy. Mormonism, too, professes belief in the Bible as the Word of God, but it has its own special inspired book, the Book of Mormon. Only Mormonism does not rest its

1. John A. O'Brien, Ph.D., *The Faith of Millions* (Huntington, Indiana: *Our Sunday Visitor,* 1938), p. 126.

case on vague and unreliable tradition, but upon the discovery, as they claim, of sacred tablets containing the new revelation. Christian Science claims to hold the Bible as divinely inspired, but Christian Science has its infallible interpreter in Mrs. Eddy. Set up any human authority beside the Sacred Scriptures, and you travel the way of heresy.

Again, whenever a second authority emerges it inevitably supersedes the primary authority. So it is in the two heresies I have mentioned; and while Rome claims firm adherence to the Scriptures, actually and practically it is the authority of the church, centered in the pope, that holds the minds of the people. "The church says so," is the Roman equivalent of our "Thus saith the Lord." True, where Scripture can be appealed to, this is done, especially when an answer to Protestants is required, but a decretal or a bull is enough for the masses of the Roman faith.

Actually, the Holy Scriptures are held in reverence as the inspired and authoritative Word of God *because the church has so decreed,* not by virtue of any authority resident in the Scriptures themselves. Father O'Brien says:

> "The Church then proceeds to declare by virtue of the teaching authority conferred upon her by Christ, as recorded in the historical document, called the New Testament, that the latter is inspired. Up until the last moment the Scriptures were appealed to simply as a historical document. It is only now, after the teaching authority of the Church has been established by the historical words of Christ that she terms the Scriptures inspired."[2]

One of the Jesuit fathers, Bailly, declared, "Without the authority of the Church I would believe St. Matthew no more

2. Ibid., p. 143.

than Titus Livius," while Cardinal Hosius, president of the great Council of Trent, affirmed that apart from the authority of the Church, the Scriptures would have no more weight than the fables of Aesop.[3] Thus the Scriptures depend for their authority on the authority of the Church. The primary authority becomes the secondary. "The first shall be last, and the last first."

Third, the pope's dominance of the interpretative functions demands a faith in man beyond his right, and it is dangerous in the extreme. How can we know that the traditions which papal infallibility has transformed into dogma are not pure fiction, or at best a mere residuum of fact with a great admixture of corruption? Let me give you a sample of what I mean.

A short time ago I became acquainted with Dr. Walter Manuel Montaño, whose thrilling story has been excellently told by B. H. Pearson in "The Monk Who Lived Again." The following incident, related in the book, was told by Dr. Montaño to a congregation in my church. It was during his monastery days, when he went by the name of Fray Luis. He was a Dominican friar, and a noted writer. On the decision of the pope to canonize a certain Beato Martin de Porres, who had been a lay member of the Dominican order four centuries before, Fray Luis was entrusted with the task of writing a history of the ancient brother, which was to be the basis of the canonization. Now very little was known about brother Martin, but he had to be elevated to the sainthood, and a history had to be written, and Fray Luis was under orders. If then, he could not write history, he could write

3. Dr. J. A. Wylie, *The Papacy* (London: Hamilton, Adams and Co., 1867), p. 172.

fiction; and, since the purpose was holy and the orders urgent, he made out a splendid story, replete with imaginary miracles. That work, which received the approval of the Dominican order, was widely read in South America, and was accepted by his holiness, the pope, as proper grounds for the proposed canonization. The infallible pope canonized Martin on the basis of a fiction. Might not the infallible pope pronounce a dogma founded on a fiction?

Infallibles ought to agree, but the Roman infallibles are consistent only if the Bible is discounted. Not only have dogmas and practices been established which are not found in Scripture, and whose sanctions are therefore referred to tradition, but others so established are positively counter to the clear teachings and spirit of Scripture, so that we have a conflict between the primary authority and the other infallibles. The proof of that must await the consideration of some of those dogmas and practices.

Chapter Two

DOES ROME SUPPRESS THE BIBLE?

"For the word of God is quick, and powerful, and sharper than any twoedged sword, piercing even to the dividing asunder of soul and spirit, and of the joints and marrow, and is a discerner of the thoughts and intents of the heart" *Hebrews* 4:12.

WITH the Bible standing as a constant challenge to its claims and teachings, it is natural that Rome should play down this primary authority while playing up its own. Indeed, Rome has gone further than a playing down game; it has engaged in a consistent and persistent suppression of the Book. That, we know, is strenuously denied by Rome's apologists.

> "But facts are chiels that winna ding,
> An' daurna be disputed."

The Church affirms her fidelity to the Holy Scriptures, making high claims to be the preserver of the Sacred Volume and the disseminator of its truths. Dr. O'Brien, for instance, seeking to acquit the Roman Church of this charge, refers to editions of the Bible issued in the Middle Ages—14 in High German before Luther sent out his translation in the common tongue, 156 in Latin, 6 in Hebrew, 10 in French, 11 in Italian, 2 in Bohemian, one each in Flemish, Limousine, and Russian; and he cites Popes Leo XIII and Benedict XV in their solicitude that the people should be acquainted with the Holy Scriptures. We might add this little sentence found at the beginning of the new Roman Catholic New Testament:

"Pope Leo XIII granted to the faithful who shall read for at least a quarter of an hour the books of the Sacred Scriptures with the veneration due to the Divine Word and as spiritual reading, an indulgence of 300 days."

But we are puzzled. If there is such anxiety to give the people the Word of God, why is there such ignorance of the Word of God on the part of the great multitude of Catholics, despite their attendance at parochial schools? Why are so few Bibles found in Catholic homes? Why, in the days of the church's power, did she assiduously hunt down those who sought to give the people the Bible in their own tongue? Why have Roman bishops and priests burned such quantities of Bibles? Why do the clergy still do all in their power to keep it from their people in parts where the church dominates, as in South America, Quebec, Spain, and Eire?

These are not straw men. Ask our missionaries from the Latin American republics whether the people there have access to the Bible. And if the Romanist replies that it is no use giving the Bible to ignorant people who cannot even read, ask him again, "Why are they so ignorant? Why cannot they read? Is not the Church the custodian of learning? Has she not been there long enough to establish universal education?" There is no such illiteracy in Protestant countries. But the lack of the Bible is not confined to the illiterate. Ask the Bible Society why it had to leave Spain. Ask the Association of Regular Baptists of Canada what kind of reception their New Testament distribution campaign is receiving in French Quebec.

But Rome will answer: You are distributing Protestant Bibles, and your translations are corrupt. That is what they said about Luther's Bible, too. Then I say to Rome, Why not distribute your own Bibles so that the Protestants will not have to distribute theirs? It is rather inappropriate for Rome to talk about the quality of Protestant translations. The official Bible of Rome is the Latin Vulgate, and what scholar would accept it as a standard? When it was issued by Sixtus V to the accompaniment of anathemas against any who would change a word of it, it was so full of corruptions that it had to be withdrawn and revised, and was reissued by Clementine VIII, still under the name of Sixtus. I believe a new revision is in process of preparation—by Protestant scholars! Before Rome talks about Protestant versions, let her produce better ones, and distribute them!

The fact is, Rome is afraid of the Bible in the speech of the people. The objection to the Protestant Bible is a mere blind. Nearly a century ago, the British and Foreign Bible Society offered to print Bibles in the Douay version without note or comment, for distribution in Ireland. The Roman clergy absolutely refused, and the Irish Catholics went without their Catholic Bible.

The contradictions of Rome's profession as regards her attitude to the Bible and its dissemination are found in official statements of her councils and popes. The Council of Toulouse, in the year 1229, made it clear that no layman might possess any portion of the Old or the New Testament. A few centuries later, when the Reformation had made its big impression on the mind of Europe, the Council of Trent seemed to make some concessions to the demand for the Bible. The people were not allowed to read the Bible, except when they received a certificate of permission from their bishop or confessor, which permission was to be granted only if said bishop or confessor were quite sure that the reading of the Sacred Volume would do the person in question no harm! Lest any should read without authorization, the sacred council decreed "That if any one shall dare to read or keep in his possession that book, without such a license, he shall not receive absolution till he has given it up to his ordinary."[1]

Now let two popes speak, both in an attempt to destroy the work of the British and Foreign Bible Society, which the Roman church has always held in fear and hatred. In the year 1816, Pope Pius VII decreed "That the Bible printed by heretics is to be numbered among other prohibited books, conformably to the rules of the index," giving as his reason, "for it is evident from experience, that the holy Scriptures, when circulated in the vulgar tongue, have through the temerity of men, produced more harm than benefit."[2] Pope Gregory XVI, later in the century, echoed former exactments: "Moreover, we confirm and renew the decrees recited above, delivered in former times by apostolic authority, against the publication, distribution, reading, and possession of books of the holy Scriptures translated into the vulgar tongue."[3] Apparently we may have the Bible, so long as it is in a language we cannot understand!

While there seems to be an easing of the suppression of the Bible in strongly democratic and largely Protestant countries, the real attitude of Rome to Bible distribution among her people is the same as ever. A group of Christians has been for some time conducting a campaign of New Testament

---

1. *The Papacy.* p. 181.
2. Ibid., p. 182.
3. Ibid., p. 182

distribution among the French Canadians of Quebec province. The Cardinal-archbishop of Quebec, Villeneuve, made plain his position when he said of these New Testaments, "This sort of literature can neither be read, kept, nor given to others in good conscience, and the best thing to do if we are insulted by having these writings sent to us is to throw them in the fire." The Bible-burning spirit is still alive in Rome. A big bonfire of Bibles is just a bit more spectacular than having single copies stuck in the stove!

The bonfires are not altogether out of date either! My friend, Dr. Paul Culley, former dean of Wheaton College, has in his possession a Bible which he rescued from a pile of Bibles, Testaments, and Christian literature collected for burning by the Roman Catholic Church in a city of the Philippines, no farther gone than the year 1939 A.D. Dr. Culley himself has told the story in the May 1939 issue of the "Philippine Evangelist." Before the "solemn" ceremony of the bonfire, there was a press exhibit of the pile of "anti-catholic" literature (prizes had been offered for collecting it!), consisting of Bibles, Testaments, Gospels, and portions. There was, by way of contrast, a Catholic display, featuring magazines from many parts of the world, lives of popes, and other items, but not a single Bible appeared in that exhibit—not even a Catholic version, nor any portion of Holy Scripture. Rome still burns Bibles!

I know the Roman apologist's answer to the stern facts of Bible-burning. It is the same as their reply to the charge of persecution: "It has never been done by the authority of the church." Apparently every act of suppression requires a special command by the pope, or else "it is not done by the authority of the church." But we have little evidence of the pope's trying to stop either the Bible-burning or the persecuting. Rome will have to assume responsibility for the consistent actions of her clergy, nor will history release the popes themselves from their active participation in these atrocities.

Another puzzle is that while Rome denies suppressing the Bible, she turns around and gives reasons for suppressing it: like a man who pleads not guilty to the charge of murder and in the same breath tells the court why he murdered his victim. Three reasons Rome gives for denying the Scriptures to the people:

(1) They cannot understand it.

(2) It would smash the Roman unity as it has Protestant unity.

(3) It is productive of atheism.

Officially a Roman Catholic is allowed to read the Bible, but just as officially he is not allowed to interpret it. Since, then, the easiest way to keep people from interpreting the Bible is to keep it out of their hands, the safest policy is suppression. That seems to be the logic of the Roman attitude.

Even the Roman priest is not permitted to seek any interpretation of Holy Scripture apart from the infallible dogmas handed to him. At his ordination he takes a solemn vow not to interpret Scripture except "according to the unanimous consent of the Holy Fathers." Support for this position is found in II Peter 1:20—"Knowing this first, that no prophecy of the scripture is of any private interpretation." That is true, and the vagaries of men are to be deplored, but Rome has forgotten that God has given to His people an infallible Interpreter of the infallible Word in the person of the Holy Spirit. It is of this the apostle John speaks when he says, "But ye have an unction from the Holy One, and ye know all things," and again, "But the anointing which ye have received of him abideth in you, and ye need not that any man teach you: but as the same anointing teacheth you of all things, and is truth, and is no lie, and even as it hath taught you, ye shall abide in him" (I John 2:20, 27). This is a complete answer both to the error of "private interpretation" and to the heresy of papal interpretation. It is the bounden duty of every Christian to submit himself to the teaching of the Holy Spirit in the Word, and the privilege of every Christian to bring every teaching of men to the judgment of the Word of God.

The Roman charge against the divisions of Protestantism is one of their strong arguments, and at first seems unanswerable to the timid, but there are several alleviating factors, to say the least, after we have admitted the tragedy of the situation. First of all, many of these Protestant factions represent the varying degrees in which different groups have thrown off the Roman heresies and practices, so that the Roman corruptions, and not the open Bible, are basically responsible for many of our differences.

Then, too, there is a difference between unity and uniformity. There are two states in which no differences are expressed—the state of the dead and the Nazi state. Pick your choice, but I shall choose the wholesome freedom of a living democracy. In this land of ours, there are political differences a-plenty, religious differences, but when Japan struck Pearl Harbor the world learned that this heterogeneous democracy was a great, solid unity. Evangelical Christianity is not a uniform system, and has many denominational expressions, but there is a living unity which is far more wonderful than any external uniformity. The prayer of our Lord for the unity of His people has not gone unanswered, despite superficial differences of practice.

On the other hand, the uniformity of Rome belies its true state. There is no such hot hatred between Protestant denominations as exists between various orders of the Roman church in their jealousy of each other. We shall not dwell on the rivalries of the Dominicans and the Franciscans, and the hatred in which the Jesuits have been held by other orders of the Roman church. Only let Rome put her own house in order before she makes propaganda of Protestantism's divisions.

Rome charges that the open Bible policy of Protestantism has produced not only divisions, but as a result, indifferentism, and then atheism. I shall answer with two questions. What made Russia officially anti-church, anti-Christian, and anti-God? Was it the Protestant's open Bible or was it a reaction to an ecclesiastical system so like Rome that one could scarcely tell them apart? Coming nearer home—what is producing the tidal wave of atheism in the South American republics, the open Bible of the Protestants or the corruptions of Rome? The Bible has a wonderful way of convincing both deceived Romanists and disillusioned atheists.

Rome claims that the Protestant attitude has come to be one of indifferentism, and contrasts that with the authoritarianism of her own system. So far as modernism, which has departed from the Bible, is concerned, that may be true, but those who cleave to the Scriptures are not indifferentists. We know that "as a man thinketh in his heart, so is he." In other words, what a man believes does matter: it determines both his character and his destiny. It is just because we are not indifferentists, because it supremely matters what a man believes, and because Rome has advanced dogmas which a man embraces at the peril of his soul, that we have undertaken the present task when our own liking should have led in very different fields of study. "He that believeth on the Son hath everlasting life: and he that believeth not the Son shall not see life; but the wrath of God abideth on him" (John 3:36). See that you believe "according to the Scripture," and not according to the traditions of men.

Chapter Three

THE PERPETUAL SACRIFICE

"For by one offering he hath perfected for ever them that are sanctified" *Hebrews* 10:14.

THE institution of the mass is very definitely held by the Roman church to be a sacrifice, and a propitiatory sacrifice at that. But we must carry back a piece to get the "build" of the doctrine. We go first to the upper room, where our Lord partook of the Last Supper with His disciples. "And as they were eating, Jesus took bread, and blessed it, and brake it, and gave it to the disciples, and said, Take, eat; this is my body. And he took the cup, and gave thanks, and gave it to them, saying, Drink ye all of it; for this is my blood of the new testament, which is shed for many for the remission of sins" (Matt. 26:26-28). The Roman teaching is that when Jesus said, "This is my body," and "this is my blood," He there and then gave His body and blood in sacrifice. The place of the actual sacrifice was not Calvary, but the upper room. At that moment He became a sacrificial victim, and from that moment He was in a dying condition, a state of victimization.

By this action a physical change came over our Lord. So that I may not unintentionally color the teaching, let me use the words of Father Richard W. Grace:[1] "That Divine High-

---

1. R. W. Grace, *The Sacrifice of Christ* (J. F. Wagner, 1937), p. 75.

Priest, who is Truth itself and a priest according to the order of Melchisedech, and who had really victimized Himself under the appearance of bread and wine, thereby unfitted His Body to hold His Blood and unfitted His Blood to abide in His Body; and, in consequence, unfitted both Body and Blood to continue in union with His human soul." Now this is the explanation of the agony in the Garden of Gethsemane. Most of us have looked upon that anguish as a foretaste of Calvary, the beginning of the desolation of soul which was to culminate in the cry of the Forsaken One on the cross. Some evangelicals indeed attribute the Gethsemane experience to the attempts of Satan to slay the Lord prematurely, before He could reach the cross. But here is something else again. His "sorrow unto death" was the direct result of that offering of Himself in the upper room under the appearances of bread and wine, and the bloody sweat was symptomatic of that physical change wrought by His self-victimization, by which His body was unfitted to contain His blood, His blood unfitted to remain in His body, and His body and blood unfitted to retain His human soul. The angel came and strengthened Him, miraculously staying the death-process until the later aspect of the sacrifice should be accomplished.

Keep in mind, please, that the Lord has already offered Himself in actual sacrifice in the upper room. What part, then, does the Cross play in the drama of sacrifice? According to the teaching, the Cross has a double significance. For one thing, it completed the sacrifice *by making it a public act*. In the second place, the Cross fixed our Lord's state as a sacrificial victim. This latter, according to the Roman teaching, is the meaning of the mighty word, "It is finished." Says Father Grace, "These words do not declare that His sacrifice was finished, but that He had finished His former, normal, earthly life and was now fixed in the state of a victim."[2] The "blood and water" which flowed from His pierced side, giving evidence of a rupture of the pericardium, are attributed to the reaction on His heart of His sacrifice of Himself in the upper room, when He offered His body and blood under the appearances of bread and wine. "When Christ victimized Himself at that Last Supper and on the cross was evidently fixed in that sacrificial state, He then began His everlasting career as the perpetual sacrifice of the New Law."[3]

This offering of Himself continues in heaven, and on earth is perpetuated in the mass. Every time the bread and the wine are consecrated on a Roman altar, Christ is sacrificed as an offering for sin as truly as we believe He was at Calvary, the only difference being that then He was offered in the true form of His humanity, while here He is offered in the form of bread and wine. Ethelred, a Cistercian superior of the 12th century in England, said to his monks, "We have no such great and evident sign of the birth of Christ as that we daily receive His body and blood at the holy altar, and that He who was once born for us of a Virgin is daily immolated in our sight."[4]

The Roman priest, then, repeats the sacrifice of Christ at every celebration of the mass. This he does, according to the teaching, in obedience to the command of the Lord Himself, "This do in remembrance of me." We have always accepted these words of the Saviour in their most simple sense, name-

---

2. Ibid., p. 108.
3. Ibid., p. 109.
4. *The Catholic Church from Within* (London: Longmans, Green, and Co., 1901), p. 170.

ly, "Eat this bread, and drink this cup, in remembrance of me." No, says Rome, that was a command given to the disciples *as priests* of the new covenant, and to all duly appointed priests who should follow them, and signifies this: "As I have now offered My body and blood under the appearances of bread and wine as a sacrifice, so must you offer in sacrifice My body and blood in every celebration of this sacrament." He was, then, imposing priestly functions upon them, and giving Himself as a perpetual victim whom they were to offer under the appearance of bread and wine. Father Grace makes much of that little word, *"This do,"* claiming that it is a sacrificial word because it is used in the Septuagint seventy-six times with reference to sacrifice.[5] Actually it is one of the commonest words in Greek, and can be used, like our own word "do," with reference to any action; and is so often used in connection with sacrifice in the Greek Old Testament because the Old Testament gives so many instructions in regard to sacrifice. The word itself proves nothing. But all that has been said amounts finally to this: since there are about four masses per second offered up in all Christendom, Christ dies, immolated on a Romish altar, four times every tick of the clock, hour after hour, day in, day out, year by year. That is the doctrine of the perpetual sacrifice.

Let me close this brief recital of the doctrine with two official declarations. The first is from the all-authoritative Council of Trent, which gave shape and expression to the faith of Rome as did the Westminster Assembly to the doctrine of Presbyterianism. "Whoever shall affirm that the sacrifice of the mass is nothing more than an act of praise and thanksgiving, or that it is simply commemorative of the sac-

5. *The Sacrifice of Christ*, p. 64.

rifice offered on the cross, and not also propitiation, or that it benefits only the person who receives it, nor ought to be offered for the living and the dead, for sins, punishments, satisfactions, and whatever besides may be requisite, let him be accursed."[6] Then, in different mood, the prayer offered with the oblation of the host says: "Accept, O Holy Father, Almighty and Eternal God, this unspotted host which I Thy unworthy servant offer unto Thee, my living and true God, for my innumerable sins, offenses, and negligences, and for all here present; as also for all faithful Christians, both living and dead; that it may avail both me and them to everlasting life. Amen."[7] (The word 'Host' is from the Latin 'hostia,' which means 'an animal slain in sacrifice, a sin offering.')

Summing up the teaching, we have these main items:

(1) When our Lord gave the bread and wine to His disciples at the Last Supper, He thereby made the sacrifice of Himself and became a victim, commanding the disciples to repeat that sacrifice with every celebration of the bread and wine.

(2) When our Lord died on the Cross, He made public the act of sacrifice actually performed in the upper room, and fixed Himself in the state of a perpetual victim.

(3) The high-priestly work of Christ consists in a continual offering of Himself in sacrifice for His people.

(4) The celebration of the mass is the continual repetition on earth of the sacrifice of Christ, under the appearances of bread and wine. The Lord Jesus is actually immolated on the Roman altar about four times every second.

---

6. Council of Trent, Sess. XXII. Cap. 1.
7. Cardinal Gibbons, *The Faith of Our Fathers* (P. J. Kenedy & Sons, New York, 110th Ed.), p. 318, (Here the cardinal uses the term "immaculate victim" instead of "unspotted host.")

(5) This perpetual sacrifice is not simply memorial, or eucharistic, but propitiatory, actually offered for sin, and to obtain eternal life for both living and dead.

What is the answer of the evangelical faith to this proposition?

First, if ever there was a fantastic interpretation of Scripture, it is surely the Roman exposition of the simple incident of the Last Supper. Only an imagination unrestrained by reality could make out of our Lord's unadorned action an article of self-immolation. We know that His whole life constituted an unblemished offering to God: we know too that in the high sense of divine appointment, He is "The Lamb slain from the foundation of the world," but to place the historic action of the sacrifice for sin in the upper room instead of at the Cross is to deny the whole tenor of Scripture and to reduce the entire function of interpretation to the level of riotous imagination. If the Cross is to be regarded as the "completion" of the sacrifice, and another point sought for the "offering" of the sacrifice, the "foundation of the world" would be more in keeping with revelation than the Last Supper. But we know that the relationship between these two is that of appointment and fulfilment, while the nearer two events are related as symbolic representation and actual accomplishment.

See how this doctrine of the sacrifice of the upper room minimizes the Cross, and that despite the publicity given the cross as a symbol in the Roman Church. Quite frankly Father Grace says, "It was not on the cross that Christ was made a victim. No, it was there that He completed His sacrifice both by its public manifestation and by finishing His passage from His former, normal, earthly life into the permanent state of a victim."[8] The death of Christ is made subservient to the institution of the Supper, which is viewed as the great moment of sacrifice: even as another Catholic writer says, "In vain would our Divine Lord have come down to save us, have been made man in the stable of Bethlehem, have died for us on the Cross, if He had not left us this Blessed Memorial of His Passion."[9] So not only the institution of the Supper, but the celebration of it, is given pre-eminence over the Cross itself. Without these, the Cross would have no efficacy.

It is scarcely necessary to say that that is not the emphasis of the New Testament. "As Moses lifted up the serpent in the wilderness, even so must the Son of man be lifted up: That whosoever believeth in him should not perish, but have eternal life" (John 3:14, 15). It is the "lifting up" on the cross that is given the emphasis. "Who his own self bare our sins in his own body on the tree" (I Pet. 2:24). "Christ *crucified*" was the apostle Paul's great emphasis. It was the "preaching of the cross" that was foolishness to those who were perishing, "but unto us which are saved it is the power of God." His strong determination, therefore, was "not to know anything among you, save Jesus Christ, and him crucified." It was on the cross that our Lord redeemed us from the curse of the law, "being made a curse for us: for it is written, Cursed is every one that hangeth on a tree" (Gal. 3:13). Till the great apostle cast all other boasting from him, saying, "God forbid that I should glory, save in the cross of our Lord Jesus Christ" (Gal. 6:14). It is the Cross that is declared to be the potent instrument of reconciliation, the

8. *The Sacrifice of Christ,* p. 175.
9. *The Catholic Church from Within,* p. 169.

blood of His Cross the agent of peace. It was at the cross that the "handwriting of ordinances that was against us" was taken away, and there the "principalities and powers" were despoiled. We shall be wise to recognize the central place of the Cross in the scheme of redemption and not shift the great act of our Lord's redeeming sacrifice elsewhere when God has placed it there!

Not only does the Roman doctrine shift the place of the actual sacrifice from the cross to the upper room, but it sweeps away the "finished work" of the Cross by its scheme of perpetual sacrifice. By a strange quirk of reasoning, Rome argues that the sacrifice of Christ was there *completed but not finished*. He must be perpetually sacrificed, invisibly in heaven, and visibly on earth in the mass. It is not the sacrifice of the Cross that is repeated, but the sacrifice of the upper room, the sacrifice of His flesh and blood under the appearances of bread and wine; and, as we have seen, that is the real act of sacrifice, according to Rome. Our Lord's own cry, "It is finished," does not refer to a finished work of atonement in His death, but the completion and fixation of the state of a perpetual victim.

Since appeal is made by Roman apologists to the epistle to the Hebrews in regard to the continuing priesthood of our Lord (and in that we heartily consent), we shall make our appeal largely to the same Scriptures in defense of the *completed and finished* sacrifice of Christ. The third verse of the first chapter is enough to establish this great truth, and I shall quote it from the revised Roman Catholic edition: "who, being the brightness of his glory and the image of his substance, and upholding all things by the word of his power, has effected man's purgation from sin and taken his seat at the right hand of the Majesty on high." Please notice the verbs here. "Being," a literal translation of the Greek present participle, and denoting continuity; "upholding," the same part of the verb, also denoting continuity of operation; then "has effected," a translation of an aorist participle in the Greek, indicating a completed action; "taken his seat," also from the aorist, which gives no hint of duration. The change from the present participles to the aorist is the significant thing here, showing that while the being and the upholding are durative, the making purgation was a completed action, and our Lord's taking His seat in glory testifies to the purification of sin being an accomplished thing, requiring no further sacrifice.

I take you now to Hebrews 7:26, 27. The Roman Catholic translation is even clearer than our King James version in this Scripture: "For it was fitting that we should have such a high priest, holy, innocent, undefiled, set apart from sinners, and become higher than the heavens. He does not need to offer sacrifices daily (as the other priests did), first for his own sins, and then for the sins of the people; for this latter he did once for all in offering up himself." If our Lord offered a "once for all" sacrifice for the sins of the people when He offered Himself, so that, as the Scripture says, He has no need to offer daily as did the priests of old, why does He have to be immolated on Roman altars four times per second "for sins, punishments, satisfactions," and the rest?

Now turn to Hebrews 9:11-14. "But Christ being come an high priest of good things to come, by a greater and more perfect tabernacle, not made with hands, that is to say, not of this building; Neither by the blood of goats and calves, but by his own blood he entered in once into the holy place, having obtained eternal redemption for us. For if the blood of bulls and of goats, and the ashes of an heifer sprinkling the unclean, sanctifieth to the purifying of the flesh: How much more shall the blood of Christ, who through the eternal Spirit offered himself without spot to God, purge your conscience from dead works to serve the living God?" Again the "once for all" entrance into the Holiest signifies a presentation needing no repetition. An offering has now been made whose efficacy is available to all. The blood of Christ, shed once on the cross, is sufficient for the cleansing of the most defiled conscience.

Again, Hebrews 9:24-28. "For Christ is not entered into the holy places made with hands, which are the figures of the true; but into heaven itself, now to appear in the presence of God for us: Nor yet that he should offer himself often, as the high priest entereth into the holy place every year with blood of others; For then must he often have suffered since the foundation of the world: but now once in the end of the world hath he appeared to put away sin by the sacrifice of himself. And as it is appointed unto men once to die, but after this the judgment: So Christ was once offered to bear the sins of many; and unto them that look for him shall he appear the second time without sin unto salvation." I cannot think how anyone, priest or layman, could read that Scripture and continue to believe in the perpetual sacrifice, the continued victimization of our Lord, either in heaven, or on the altar of the mass.

But go on into the 10th chapter and read the first 14 verses. Here we learn that, once perfected, we need no more offering for sin, and we are also told that He has perfected us by the one offering of Himself. The perpetual sacrifice is a positive denial of the efficacy of the "once for all" sacrifice. The Romanists hold, of course, that their sacrifice of the mass is the *same* sacrifice, not other than that which our Lord Himself offered. But in this Scripture the sacrifices of Israel are spoken of as identical. The repetition marked the first and all successive sacrifices as ineffectual. To offer the "Same" sacrifice is to account its first offering ineffectual, so the whole system of the mass blasphemes the one perfect, all-sufficient offering of our Lord, by which we have been sanctified and given a standing of perfection before a holy God.

Let me turn to Romans for a last reference in this regard —a Scripture which gives an annihilating answer to the Roman position. "Now if we be dead with Christ, we believe that we shall also live with him: Knowing that Christ being raised from the dead dieth no more; death hath no more dominion over him. For in that he died, he died unto sin once: but in that he liveth, he liveth unto God" (Rom. 6:8-10). What shall we do with the four times per second immolation of Christ on Roman altars in view of this declaration that He "dieth no more"? We shall regard such a teaching as one of the most shocking blasphemies of the Christian age, and turn with new fervor of trust and gratitude to that one sacrifice of the Cross by which our redemption was forever won, in which we see the remission of our sins and our eternal life

> "Lifted up was He to die;
> 'It is finished!'—was His cry:
> Now in heaven, exalted high:—
> Hallelujah! What a Saviour!"

Chapter Four

THE DOGMA OF TRANSUBSTANTIATION

"For as often as ye eat this bread, and drink this cup, ye do shew the Lord's death till he come" *I Corinthians* 11:26.

WE have thus far been focusing our thought particularly on the sacrifice of the mass, and should now consider the sacrament which so closely accompanies it—the sacrament of the holy eucharist. The difference between the sacrifice and the sacrament must be kept in mind. The sacrifice is presented to God as a propitiatory offering for sin, to obtain absolution and other spiritual benefits. In the sacrament the worshipper receives something which imparts grace, involving union with God in the person of the victim. The Catholic Catechism defines the difference as the Roman church views it. "How is the Sacrament of the Holy Eucharist distinguished from the Sacrifice? The Sacrament of the Eucharist is distinguished from the Sacrifice: (1) because the Sacrament is completed by the Consecration and remains, whereas the whole idea of sacrifice consists in its being offered up — hence the Sacred Host, when in the Tabernacle or when taken to the sick, is to be regarded as a Sacrament and not as a Sacrifice; (2) because the Sacrament is the cause of merit in those who receive it and is for the profit of their souls, whereas the Sacrifice is not only a source of merit but also has the power of making satisfaction."[1]

1. Cardinal Gasparri, *The Catholic Catechism,* p. 170   (Authorized translation of Hugh Pope, O. P.)

The same elements appear in both sacrifice and sacrament
—the bread and the wine: the one consecration constitutes
these a fit object for both sacrifice and sacrament, the body
and blood of Christ to be offered on the altar to God as a
true sacrifice for sin, the same body and blood of Christ to
be received by the worshipper as a communion. Now the
act of consecration does not merely hallow the bread and wine
as sacred symbols of the body and blood of our Lord. The
holy eucharist is more than a memorial supper. It is here
that the dogma of the "Real Presence" enters. The Catechism
declares: "The Sacrament of the Holy Eucharist is a Sacrament instituted by Christ wherein Jesus Christ Himself, the
Author of grace, is truly, really, and substantially contained
under the appearances of bread and wine for the spiritual re-
freshment of our souls."[2] It is the act of consecration that
determines the "Real Presence." "When the priest in the
Mass pronounces the words of consecration over the bread
and wine, The Body and Blood of our Lord Jesus Christ,
together with His Soul and His Godhead, become truly,
really, and substantially present under the appearances of
bread and wine."[3]

It is not a matter, either, of our Lord entering into the
bread and wine in some mystical fashion. The bread and
wine are actually changed into the very flesh and blood of the
Redeemer. This change is called transubstantiation, and is
defined thus: "When Jesus Christ pronounced the words of
consecration over the bread and wine, there took place a
wonderful and unique change of the whole substance of the
bread into the Body and of the whole substance of the wine

2. Ibid., p. 169.
3. Ibid., p. 165.

into the Blood of Jesus Christ, although the appearances of bread and wine remained."[4] This same change is wrought every time a priest consecrates bread and wine at the altar. The official dictum of the Council of Trent on this subject is as follows: "Trent, Sess. XIII, *Decretum de sanctissima Eucharistia,* cap. IV: 'But since Christ our Redeemer said that that was truly His Body which He was offering up under the appearance of bread, it has always been the conviction of the Church of God—and this Holy Synod declares it anew—that by the consecration of the bread and wine the entire substance of bread is converted into the substance of the Body of Christ our Lord, and the entire substance of wine into the substance of His Blood, which conversion is by the Catholic Church fittingly and rightly termed trans-substantiation.' "[5]

Roman Catholics are very particular how this doctrine is stated. Dr. Alexander Whyte wrote a handbook on the Presbyterian Shorter Catechism. Commenting on the statement dealing with the Lord's Supper, which says that we are, "not after a corporal or carnal manner, but by faith, made partakers of His body and blood," Dr. Whyte suggested, "This is directed against the Popish doctrine of transubstantiation. According to that doctrine the bread and wine are changed into the very flesh and blood of Christ, so that all communicants literally and physically eat the flesh and drink the blood of Christ." The author of the handbook sent a copy to Newman, the former Anglican priest turned Roman and elevated to the high rank of Cardinal, with whom Dr. Whyte remained in personal friendship till the death of the aged cleric. The cardinal took exception to the wording I have just

---

4. Ibid., p. 163.
5. Ibid., p. 370.

quoted, so the good Presbyterian asked the cardinal to suggest a statement which would truly represent the Roman position. Alexander Whyte incorporated Newman's statement into his second edition, as follows: "According to this doctrine, 'the substance of the bread and wine is converted into the substance of the very flesh and blood of Christ, so that all communicants literally and substantially partake of His flesh and blood.'"[6] There is little to choose from, but by using the terms of the Romanists themselves we shall avoid the least danger of misrepresentation.

Of course, the appearances of the bread and wine remain, what are called the accidents, that is, the shape, size, color, weight, taste, and everything that touches the senses. Nevertheless the substance is not bread, nor wine, but the flesh and blood of Jesus Christ. The Roman Catholic is taught to deny his senses in this matter and accept that which looks, feels, smells, and tastes like bread and wine as something else, the substance of these having been changed into the substance of the body and blood of Christ. Cyril of Jerusalem therefore teaches in his Catecheses: "Judge not by the taste but by faith, put away hesitation and be certain that ye have been honored with the gift of the Body and Blood of Christ. Taught thus; imbued with this most sure faith that what seems bread is not bread—though to the sense of taste it may be so—but is the body of Christ; that what seems wine is not wine—though to the taste it may seem so—but is the Blood of Christ—in this faith strengthen thy heart."[7]

Not only is this faith encouraged, but it is demanded, and

6. Barbour, *The Life of Alexander Whyte* (New York: George H Doran, 1925), p. 243.
7. Catholic Catechism, p. 373

a curse pronounced on all who receive it not. Here is the decree of the Council of Trent: "If anyone shall say that in the Most Holy Sacrament of the Eucharist there remains the substance of bread and wine together with the Body and Blood of our Lord Jesus Christ, and shall deny that marvelous and unique conversion of the entire substance of the bread into His Body, and of the entire substance of wine into His Blood, while the species of bread and wine alone remain, a conversion which the Catholic Church most fittingly terms transubstantiation, let him be anathema."[8] Moreover, there is no salvation for anyone outside the church which holds and teaches this doctrine of transubstantiation. So said the Lateran Council of 1215, in its decree against the Albigenses: "There is one universal Church of the faithful outside which absolutely no one is saved, in which Jesus Christ Himself is both Priest and Victim, whose Body and Blood are truly contained in the Sacrament of the altar under the appearances of bread and wine, the bread and the wine being by the Divine power trans-substantiated into His Body and Blood, so that for the perfecting of the mystery of unity we may receive of Him what He took from us."[9]

The Romanists defend this dogma by an appeal to that mystical statement of our Lord in John 6:51-56 in which He presents Himself as the bread of life; and also to the words of the institution, "This is my body—this is my blood." With regard to the former passage, they hold that our Lord was promising a literal giving of His flesh and blood for eating and drinking unto life everlasting; that He fulfilled this promise to the disciples in the upper room, where they ate

8. Ibid., p. 376.
9. Ibid., p. 375.

the flesh and drank the blood of the Lord under the appearances of bread and wine; and that in like manner His flesh and blood are eaten and drunk in the sacrament of the Holy Eucharist as a means of obtaining life everlasting and union with God in Christ. Again, the words, "this is my body," and "this is my blood," are to be taken in utter literalness, the verb being used to signify complete identity.

We have stated the dogma of Rome, and I scarcely need to declare our disagreement. John Wyclif was cited by the Council of Constance (1414-1418) for his three protestations against the doctrine of transubstantiation:

"(1) The material substance of bread, and similarly the material substance of wine, remain in the Sacrament of the altar.

"(2) The accidents of bread do not remain without a subject in the said Sacrament.

"(3) Christ is not in the said Sacrament identically and really in His own corporal presence."[10]

We might express our protest against the Roman doctrine in other terms, but let us see whether we can sustain the evangelical position against the popish one.

First, we are asked to believe a miracle for which there is not a scrap of evidence. Bible miracles are not of that order, but have themselves evidential value, being wrought as aids to faith, not as stumbling-blocks. When God turned Moses' rod into a serpent, it had not only the substance of a serpent, but all the marks and tokens of a serpent, so that even Moses fled from it. When God turned the water of Egypt into blood, it did not retain the accidents of water. The Egyptians could not drink it. When our Lord turned the water into

10. Ibid., p. 376.

wine at Cana, the ruler of the feast did not have to lay down a dogma to the guests that what looked like, tasted like, and was odorless like water was really very fine wine. When lame men were healed, they did not carry the limping appearance of lame men around with them. Some Roman Catholics will answer that this is "trifling with the things of God." Not so. On the contrary, if God did what Rome affirms in the eucharist, God would be trifling with human reason, that gift of the Creator which is one of the marks of the divine image in man. The faith unto salvation which God demands is not a blind faith: it is a faith supported by ample evidence in creation, in history, in providence, in experience. Only Rome asks for a blinding of the reason for belief in her dogmas.

In only one form is our Lord Jesus represented in all His appearings to men, and that is "like unto the Son of man." Even when He is spoken of as an angel, the form is that of a man. This is true both in the Christophanies of the Old Testament and in the post-ascension appearings. When He passed by Elijah on Mount Horeb, the mighty wind, the shivering earthquake, and the fire betokened His presence, but "the Lord was not in the wind . . . the Lord was not in the earthquake . . . the Lord was not in the fire" (I Kings 19:11,12). Our Lord has humbled Himself to enter into our humanity, but Rome has humbled Him still further into the form of inanimate bread and wine to be eaten and drunk by sinners. Of course, if a rat were accidentally to find the wafer, it would magically become no longer Christ but return to its former substance of bread! No, no! the humiliation of our Lord to the death of the Cross is not thus rewarded with perpetual humiliation on Roman altars, but with perpetual exaltation. "Wherefore God also hath highly exalted Him," not in the elevation of the host for idolatrous worship, but "at His own right hand in the heavenlies." Nor is He at the same time exalted in heaven and degraded on earth. The day of His humiliation is past. Men may spurn Him, scoff at Him, blaspheme Him, but they can no more humiliate Him whom God has exalted far above all heavens, a Prince and a Saviour.

But how shall we regard those statements of our Lord, in His Galilee address on the bread of life and in the institution of the supper, upon which Rome's apologists depend for a defense of their doctrine? Let us read the wonderful verses in John 6:51-59: "I am the living bread which came down from heaven: if any man eat of this bread, he shall live for ever: and the bread that I will give is my flesh, which I will give for the life of the world. The Jews therefore strove among themselves, saying, How can this man give us his flesh to eat? Then Jesus said unto them, Verily, verily, I say unto you, Except ye eat the flesh of the Son of man, and drink his blood, ye have no life in you. Whoso eateth my flesh, and drinketh my blood, hath eternal life; and I will raise him up at the last day. For my flesh is meat indeed, and my blood is drink indeed. He that eateth my flesh, and drinketh my blood, dwelleth in me, and I in him. As the living Father hath sent me, and I live by the Father: so he that eateth me, even he shall live by me. This is that bread which came down from heaven: not as your fathers did eat manna, and are dead: he that eateth of this bread shall live forever. These things said he in the synagogue, as he taught in Capernaum."

"How can this man give us his flesh to eat?" asked the multitude. We have heard Rome's answer. Let us hear

Christ's own answer. He presents a triple proposition regarding eating His flesh and drinking His blood. Negatively, eating the flesh and drinking the blood of the Son of man is the "sine qua non" of life for men (vs. 53). Positively, their partaking of the flesh and blood of the Lord Jesus imparts eternal life and assures a place in the resurrection of life and blessedness (vs. 54). Further, eating and drinking of this sacred meat is the means of communion, through mutual indwelling (vs. 56). But what does it mean to eat the flesh and drink the blood of the Son of man? We do not have to go far afield for an explanation of this mystical language. Eating is to satisfy hunger; drinking is to quench thirst. The satisfying meat and drink are His flesh and blood. How do we eat and drink of these? He has Himself told us in this very chapter, in verse 35: "He that *cometh to me* shall never hunger; and he that *believeth on me* shall never thirst." If coming to Him is the end of hunger, and believing on Him the end of thirst, then the coming and the believing are the eating and the drinking.[11] But it is a coming to Him and a believing on Him *as the crucified One,* the sacrificed One. who *in His death* accomplished all that the ancient altar taught of substitution, atonement, and reconciliation. That sacrifice we recall at every partaking of the simple communion feast, and there we renew our faith and love.

When many of our Lord's disciples, who thought only in terms of an earthly Messiah, heard this mystical language with its strong flavor of the altar and sacrifice, they were offended, saying, "This is a repulsive saying." Now listen to

---

11. Dr. Henry M. Woods quotes a Spanish priest, Maldonado, as saying in this regard: "Do not prepare your teeth and your belly for it, but *believe* in Him, and you have *eaten* Him." That is evangelical, not Roman, teaching!

our Lord's answer: "Doth this offend you? What and if ye shall see the Son of man ascend up where he was before? It is the spirit that quickeneth; the flesh profiteth nothing: the words that I speak unto you, they are spirit, and they are life" (vv. 61-63). He was talking, He declared, not in physical or sacramental terms, but spiritual. It is not eating the substance of His flesh that gives life, nor drinking the substance of His blood. He has spoken in the language of sacrifice, and when we embrace His finished work for us, we enter into the benefits of His sacrifice: that is eating His flesh and drinking His blood. There is nothing carnal about it.

Now we come to the strong argument of Rome. Our Lord said, "This is my body," and "This is my blood," and what right have we to turn from or alter these plain statements? That sounds like good reasoning, but it is not as easy as that. The verb in the Greek, *esti,* is the counterpart of our verb "to be," and is used with as varied meanings as our own. In the unabridged Liddell and Scott lexicon, I read this under *eimi Bi*—"to be, the Copula connecting the predicate with the subject, both being in the same case:—this is the commonest usage;—sometimes the simpler sense of *to be* passes into that of *to amount to, to signify, import*—especially in the phrase tout' esti, hoc est." Now that is the very structure used here, both in the Greek text and in the Latin Vulgate. So the word sometimes means "To signify," especially in this structure, *without departing from a literal sense*. If this is a recognized usage, why should it be denied to our Lord, when that is the sensible sense of the phrase? If we must stick to the stern literalness that Rome demands in this connection, we shall find ourselves in difficulties. "This cup is the new testament," said Jesus, here omitting the verb and so making the identity the stronger. No one can deny that here we have figurative language. For one thing, the cup is put for the contents, and certainly neither the cup nor its contents constituted the covenant, but symbolized it. Zwingli, when arguing this point in Zurich, referred to the parallel Old Testament institution of the Passover, where it is said in Exodus 12:11 concerning the lamb, "Ye shall eat it in haste: it is the Lord's passover." The same verb is here used in the Septuagint as in the institutional passage in the New Testament, and there is no doubt about its use in the sense of "signify." The Roman demand for the literal sense here is both baseless and senseless.

But now I want to present a blatant inconsistency in the Roman position. As most of you probably know, the communicants in the Roman church receive only the bread of communion, the cup being kept for the priest. The law banning the cup to the laity was given by the Council of Constance in 1414, and confirmed by the Council of Trent, so often referred to. Now if the bread is the very flesh of Christ, and the wine His very blood, why should the laity be barred from the latter when our Lord said, "Except ye eat the flesh of the Son of man, *and drink his blood,* ye have no life in you" (John 6:53)? Rome has her answer, in the form of another dogma, namely, concomitance. Let the Council of Trent again give its infallible dictum: "It has always been the belief of the Church that immediately after the Consecration the true Body of our Lord as well as His true Blood, under the appearances of bread and wine, His soul also and His Godhead, are there; the Body under the appearance of bread, the Blood under the appearance of wine by force of the very words used, but the Body too under the appearance of wine, and the Blood under the appearance of bread, and the soul as well under either, by force of that natural connection and concomitance whereby the parts of Christ our Lord, who has now risen from the dead to die no more, are knit together; His Godhead also, by reason of His wonderful hypostatic union with His soul and body. Whence it is most true that as much is contained under either species as under both; for the whole and entire Christ is under the appearance of bread and under every particle of those species, the same, too, under the species of wine and of its every drop. If anyone shall deny that in the Venerable Sacrament of the Eucharist the entire Christ is contained under either species and under every particle of either when separated, let him be anathema."[12] In keeping with this, an English Catholic writes: "Not only do we receive Him whole and entire under either species, but we receive, by what is called concomitance, the Soul and Divinity of our Divine Saviour as well."[13] Dr. John O'Brien enumerates the reasons given by the Council of Trent for the withholding of the cup from the laity: "the danger of spilling the Precious Blood; the difficulty of reserving the sacrament under the species of wine; and the danger to health from partaking of a chalice touched by infected lips."[14] In other words, our Blessed Lord did not quite know what He was up to, and the Church had to improve upon His instruction. Why did the Lord give the sacrament in a form fraught with such danger and difficulty? See how Rome has both added to and taken from the words of the Lord. He said of the bread, "It is my body," but Rome says, "It is body, blood, soul and divinity." Jesus says of the cup, "It is my blood," but Rome says, "It is blood, body, soul and divinity." Rome

---

12. Ibid., p. 380
13. *The Catholic Church from Within*, p. 172.
14. *The Faith of Millions*, p. 223

must needs correct the Lord's teaching. Then Jesus says, "This do," both of the bread and of the cup, while the apostle Paul gives by the word of the Lord, "As often as ye eat this bread, *and* drink this cup, ye do show the Lord's death till he come" (I Cor. 11:26). But Rome will force her communicants to a partial obedience, assuring them that they are receiving all in the part.

It remains to say a word about the elevation of the host, at which all Catholics bow in adoration. It is no ordinary reverence that is given to the consecrated wafer, but the worship of *latria,* the worship which is given to God alone, for this wafer has become very God. We call it idolatry. The Romanist, of course, will answer that he is not worshipping an image or idol, but the Lord Jesus Christ under the appearance of bread. That exactly is the essence of idolatry—to worship God under any appearance whatsoever. When Aaron made the golden calf in the wilderness and said to the people, "These be thy gods, O Israel, which brought thee up out of the land of Egypt" (Exod. 32:4), both Aaron and the people knew that this calf, which they had seen made before their eyes, was not God, nor had it brought them out of Egypt— rather they had brought it out in the form of earrings. But by the consecration of that calf they believed that God was present in it, and they worshipped God under the appearance of the calf. But God would not be identified with it, and judged them for idolatry. Even the heathen do not profess to worship stones and trees, but the spirits identified with them. And the attempt to worship God under any species is pure idolatry. "Thou shalt not make unto thee any graven image, or any likeness of anything that is in heaven above, or that is in the earth beneath, or that is in the water under the earth. Thou shalt not bow down thyself to them, nor serve them" (Exod. 20:4, 5a).[15] That is just what Rome does, bowing down before a piece of bread transformed into a god. There is no more blatant idolatry in all heathendom than the idolatry of the mass. So, then, the very heart of the whole Roman system is a great blasphemy, a shocking idolatry.

---

15. It is significant that Rome omits this commandment from her catechism, and splits the last two to make up the number ten.

Chapter Five

THE ROMAN PRIESTHOOD

"But Jesus called them unto him, and said, Ye know that
the princes of the Gentiles exercise dominion over them,
and they that are great exercise authority upon them.
But it shall not be so among you: but whosoever will
be great among you, let him be your minister; And whosoever will be chief among you, let him be your servant:
Even as the Son of man came not to be ministered unto,
but to minister, and to give his life a ransom for many"
Matthew 20:25-28.

ROME calls her ministers priests. Other communions do
the same, but evangelicals among them do not apply the
sacramental connotation to the term that Rome does, while
most Protestant bodies shrink from the term itself as referring
to a clerical class.

In the New Testament the Christian minister is not once
given this title. The three categories that bear it are: the
priests of the Old Testament order, which was still in existence in the days of Christ, and continued to function, although rejected of God, till the fall of Jerusalem; our Lord
Jesus Himself, who in His exaltation at God's right hand is
"a priest for ever after the order of Melchisedec"; and all believers, who are designated "a kingdom of priests," "a royal
priesthood," whose function now and hereafter is "to offer up
spiritual sacrifices, acceptable to God by Jesus Christ" (I Pet.

2:5). A priestly class within the ranks of the redeemed is not found in the New Testament.

The New Testament minister is variously designated in Scripture. The word "minister" is a translation of three different Greek terms. One is *leitourgos* from which we derive our word liturgy. It originally meant one who did service for the state in some official capacity, and so came over into the church to indicate one serving God in a particular office. Yet its uses in the New Testament are varied. Appearing five times, it refers once to civil rulers, once to Paul as a minister of Christ, once to Epaphroditus who was sent to Paul from the church in Philippi with their gift to the apostle, once to angels, and once to our Lord in His priestly character. Only once, then, does this title carry the thought of priestly functions, and that when applied to Christ Himself (Heb. 8:2). It is scarcely necessary to deal with the associated words, which also carry divers applications, but never fasten distinctly priestly duties upon a class within the church.

The second term, *hupéretés*, signifies originally an oarsman in a galley, and then an assistant. It is frequently translated "officer," and sometimes "servant." Four times it is used in the New Testament of Christians; once of the disciples when Jesus said that they would fight if His kingdom were of this world; once of John Mark, who accompanied Barnabas and Paul as their assistant; once of Paul, where the title is joined to that of witness; once of Paul, Apollos, and Peter, when Paul was condemning the schism that had arisen in Corinth over their names, as if they were rivals instead of co-operating servants of the Lord. Once again, no sign of a priesthood appears under this term.

The third is *diakonos,* from which we have our word

deacon. Again there is a variety of usages. We read of "deacons of Satan," deacons of men, deacons of God, and deacons of the church. Christ Himself is referred to as a "deacon of the circumcision." Sometimes the functions are civil, sometimes domestic, sometimes religious, but there is no case where it is clearly priestly.

Apart from these terms which are frequently translated "minister" in our version, the New Testament ministers have other designations. "Elder" and "bishop" are two of these. They would seem to signify the one office, for when Paul called together the "elders" of the church at Ephesus, he addressed them as those whom the Holy Spirit had appointed "bishops" of the flock. John and Peter called themselves elders. In this regard Peter, whom Rome has raised to the place of primacy as the first pope, used a lovely term. Addressing the elders, he called himself the *sunpresbuteros,* "elder along with," so taking his place not simply on a par with the other apostles, but on a level with the common run of elders in the church. Whatever leadership he had in the infant church, he was only *primus inter pares.* The title "bishop" denotes the administrative function of oversight, the title "elder" the mature character which should mark the office. It is clear, too, that there was a plurality of elders, or bishops, in each church, not one bishop over many churches. The episcopate as we now know it was a post-apostolic development.

Again, the ministry of the New Testament church included prophets, evangelists, pastors, and teachers, these terms referring not to the offices held but to the ministries performed. One person might perform several of these ministries, even as today, and might or might not hold office as elder or bishop. But in all this wide variety of terminology and function, the priestly conception is strangely absent. It is equally wanting in the accounts of apostolic activity and in the apostolic teachings. There is no trace of the apostles taking over, or instructing others to take over, some New Testament counterpart of the Levitical priesthood. The apostles continued for a time to participate in the ritual of the temple, even to bringing offerings, but they never regarded themselves as successors of the Jewish priests. Once the apostle Paul uses the language of the altar to depict his spirit of self-sacrifice on behalf of the saints: "Yea, and if I be offered upon the sacrifice and service of your faith, I joy, and rejoice with you all" (Phil. 2:17). It would be straining the passage to distortion to read into it anything of a professional priesthood.

To the Roman priest are attributed two prerogatives which give him the dominating place he holds in the lives of the people. Theologically these are stated as "the jurisdiction over the natural and over the mystical Body of Christ."[1] Jurisdiction over the natural body of Christ means the consecration of the sacrament of the altar in which the bread becomes, at the word of the priest, the very flesh of our Lord: that is, the whole substance of the bread becomes the whole substance of the body of Christ. The jurisdiction of the mystical Body of Christ, namely, the church, signifies the priest's power to give absolution, to forgive sin.

We have already considered the question of the substantial change of the bread and wine into the very flesh and blood of Christ. We return to it only to consider what extravagant exaltation this gives to the Roman priest.

---

1. Cardinal H. E. Manning, *Eternal Priesthood* (Burns, 1883), p. 12.

In Montreal I obtained a copy of a booklet written for the edification of the faithful, and entitled "The Priest." It carries the imprimatur of the Archbishop of Ottawa. The author does not give his name, but devotes a good portion of the little volume to quotations from a French venerable, since he feels himself altogether unworthy to speak on the exalted topic of a fellow-sinner who has received holy orders. "In order to explain to you what the priest is, and to speak to you in a manner befitting the subject, my life would need to be purified with a burning coal, as the angel purified those of the prophet." Then he proceeds to quote from an address delivered by the venerable J. B. M. Vianney, Curé d' Ars, to a throng of pilgrims. Here are a few of the sentences quoted:

"Where there is no priest there is no sacrifice, and where there is no sacrifice there is no religion."

"Without the priest the death and passion of our Lord would be of no avail to us."

"See the power of the priest! By one word from his lips, he changes a piece of bread into a God! A greater feat than the creation of a world."

After that you do not wonder at these others:

"If I were to meet a priest and an angel, I would salute the priest before saluting the angel. The angel is a friend of God, but the priest holds the place of God."

"Next to God Himself, the priest is everything."

"Did we understand him and appreciate him in this life, we should die, not of fear, but of love - - -."

John the Baptist said concerning our blessed Lord, "He must increase, but I must decrease." That order is reversed in the case of the Roman priest. With the exaltation of the priest comes the humiliation of the Lord. That was seen in connection with the perpetual sacrifice, but listen to the bold statement of Cardinal Manning as he writes about the powers of the priesthood: "The incarnation was a descent which had many degrees. He emptied Himself by veiling His glory; He took the form of a servant; He was made man; He humbled Himself; and that to death; and to die in ignominy. Here are six degrees of humiliation. And *as if these were not enough, He perpetuates His humility in the Blessed Sacrament, and places Himself in the hands of His creatures, and is bid, morning by morning, by their word to be present upon the altar;* and is by them lifted up, and carried to and fro, and, in the end, He is received by the worthy and by the unworthy. In this divine manner *He subjects Himself to the jurisdiction of His priests now - - -*"[2] The apostle Paul invited the Lord to command him: the Lord is at the beck and call of the Roman priest.

The power of the priest is further enhanced by his jurisdiction over the mystical Body of Christ, or his power to forgive sins. As his power to bring Christ down upon the altar is said to have been bestowed by our Lord's words in the upper room, "This do in remembrance of me," so the prerogative of absolution was declared in the upper room after the resurrection, when the Lord, breathing upon them, said: "Receive ye the Holy Ghost: Whose soever sins ye remit, they are remitted unto them; and whose soever sins ye retain, they are retained" (John 20:22, 23). To like purpose were the words to Simon Peter at Caeserea Philippi, "Whatsoever thou shalt bind on earth shall be bound in heaven: and whatsoever thou shalt loose on earth shall be loosed in heaven" (Matt. 16:19). Confessedly these are difficult passages, and involve more

---

2. Ibid., p. 13 (italics ours).

than one question of unending controversy. In the first place, it is a question whether these words were spoken to Peter and his successors, and to the apostles and their successors, or whether they conferred peculiar rights and prerogatives on the apostles alone. But suppose we grant that Peter and his fellow-apostles were to have successors in the church who should enjoy all their powers and privileges, it is certain that these words did not grant to the successors more than they gave to the original recipients. It will be safe to go no farther in the exercise of the rights involved than did the apostles. Is there, then, a single instance recorded in all the New Testament of an apostle forgiving sins in the manner practiced by the priests of the church of Rome? There is not the faintest suggestion of it. Did Peter "give absolution" to Cornelius, or Paul to the Philippian jailor? They preached to them salvation and the forgiveness of sins and opened the way for them by their proclamation. Peter discerned the sin of Ananias and Sapphira and pronounced God's judgment on it; Paul discerned the wickedness of Elymas and declared sentence upon it. Peter rebuked the iniquity of Simon of Samaria and bade him repent lest evil should befall him. Paul charged the church at Corinth to excommunicate the braggart adulterer, but when the sinner was broken to repentance he bade the church receive him again, saying, "To whom ye forgive anything, I forgive also: for what I also have forgiven, if I have forgiven anything, for your sakes have I forgiven it in the presence of Christ" (II Cor. 2:10 R.V.). Here the apostle does not use the great theological word for forgiveness or remission of sins, but a word signifying "to act graciously." In no place do we find the apostles calling for auricular confession and giving absolution. The practice is foreign to the New Testament.

There is indeed a binding and a loosing incumbent on the church. I speak of the matter of discipline, the very matter that Paul dealt with in the Corinthian church. When a church, seeking the mind of the Spirit, imposes discipline upon a recalcitrant, unrepentent member, that action is accepted and bound in heaven: when that same church withdraws the disciplinary measures because of manifest repentance, that loosing is honored in heaven. But that is a far cry from the authoritative absolution of the Roman priest.

The sacrament of penance, the name given by Rome to this practice of confession and absolution, puts the priest into a relation with the soul which belongs only to Christ. It makes him a mediator between God and that soul. The catechism states this quite boldly: "The dignity of the priesthood is very great, for the priest is the minister of Christ and the dispenser of the mysteries of God; he is a mediator between God and man, with power over the real as well as the mystical Body of Christ."[3] Then, with an utter disregard for the blatant contradiction, it goes on, "Christ is the 'One Mediator of God and men'; that is, He alone is the Mediator of redemption. But the priest, acting in the person of Christ, applies to men the fruits of that redemption and is thus rightly called a mediator." Behold how the sinner is shut up to do business with a fellow-sinner who steps between him and the one great divine Mediator, our Advocate with God and the fountain of all blessing! If the confessional were a voluntary institution, established for purposes of counsel and help, it could be of inestimable value. But to shut souls up to a confession of their sins to a fellow-mortal as the only

3. Catholic Catechism, p. 189.

agent of forgiveness, is to rob God of His glory and put it upon a sinner.

> "Such vile offenses to forgive,
> Such guilty, daring worms to spare,
> This is Thy grand prerogative,
> And in the honor none shall share;
> Who is a pardoning God like Thee,
> Or who has grace so rich and free?"

With all its profession of being a Christian church, Rome has an insidious way of pointing men to someone other than Christ. In Montreal there is an immense shrine built in honor of Brother André, and dedicated to the patron saint of the city, Joseph, husband of Mary. At the entrance is a statue of the saint, and on the front this motto in Latin, *Ite ad Joseph.* Now the subtlety of it all is that these words were spoken of another Joseph altogether, the Joseph who was sold into Egypt, and they were addressed by Pharaoh to the Egyptians who came to him for corn during the famine. By such a trick the "faithful" are directed to Joseph. Then the devotional literature of Rome carries this perversion: "Come unto Mary, all ye that labor and are heavy laden, and she will give you rest." So the unwary are turned aside from Him who spoke these precious words of invitation. Now we see the intrusion of the priest as mediator, trading with a forgiveness which is the sole prerogative of the God-man, our Lord Jesus Christ. The Jews were right in their question, "Who can forgive sins but God alone?"—if only they had seen God in the Son of man, our blessed Lord.

The Roman forgiveness is not only a fiction and a fallacy, but it is laden with the dynamite of iniquity. I have no desire to expatiate on what have been called "the atrocities of the confessional," but only to indicate that the system is charged with peril. After all, priests are only men, made of common clay, and they are deprived of the normal associations open to other men. Dr. Pusey, one of the leading Romanizers in the Church of England in the nineteenth century, admitted the grave disorders among the clergy of his own communion who had embraced the Roman practices of celibacy and the confessional. "It is a sad sight," he writes in his book on Confession, "to see confessors giving their whole morning to young women devotees, while they dismiss men or married women"—"a great desire of one another's society arises, and thus *spiritualis devotio convertibur in carnalem.* How many good priests have been the victims of such affections, begun in piety, and have at last lost both piety and God Himself!" I am sure Romanists are no stronger than Romanizers to withstand the temptations here indicated.

The Scriptures exhort us: "Whatsoever things are true, whatsoever things are honest, whatsoever things are just, whatsoever things are pure, whatsoever things are lovely, whatsoever things are of good report; if there be any virtue, and if there be any praise, think on these things" (Phil. 4:8). For a large portion of his time a confessor-priest must let his mind dwell on things that are untrue, dishonest, unjust, impure, unlovely, of bad report, without virtue and without praise. Moreover he must become expert in dragging out the worst. No wonder if his mind becomes sordid, and what at first appalled him turn to meat for a debased mental appetite. I would not charge that this universally happens, but no one can paddle in foul streams without being muddied.

The very secrecy of the confessional, which is one of the boasts of Rome, is fraught with its own dangers. An ex-priest of the Roman church in Ireland gave this testimony in a pamphlet published in 1838—"The most awful of all considerations is this, that through the confessional I have been frequently apprized of intended assassinations and most diabolical conspiracies; and still, from the ungodly injunctions of secrecy in the Romish creed, lest, as Peter Dens says, the confessional should become odious, I dared not give the slightest intimation to the marked out victims of slaughter."[4] Peter Dens, referred to in this quotation, is one of Rome's chief authorities on the confessional, a standard for the priesthood. In his manual he asks the question, "What answer ought a Confessor to give, when questioned about a truth which he knows from sacramental confession only?" The reply is, "He ought to answer that he does not know, and if necessary, confirm it by an oath." Alphonso Liguori, another *authority*, adds blasphemy to hypocrisy. Dealing with the case of a priest brought as a witness to court, he says, "A priest is brought as a witness only as a man; and therefore without injury to conscience he can swear that he does not know things which he knows only as God." Thus priests are taught to perjure themselves "without injury to conscience!"

The confession to which Scripture calls us knows none of the moral perversions of the Roman sacrament. When we read, "If we confess our sins, he is faithful and just to forgive us our sins, and to cleanse us from all unrighteousness" (I John 1:9), we are not being invited to deal with some fellow-sinner whom "holy orders" has exalted to the place of a God, but to Him who had "power on earth to forgive sins," and who, from the throne, ministers the cleansing of His own blood. I like the reply of the old woman to the

---

4. *The Papacy*, p. 329, footnote.

priest who made a last effort to bring her back into the "church" as she lay dying. "I have come to forgive your sins," he said to her. "Show me your hands," the aged saint answered; then, when the astonished priest showed his hands, she said; "You cannot forgive my sins. The Man who forgives my sins has the marks of nails in His hands." Yes, beloved, "through *this* man is preached unto you the forgiveness of sins" (Acts 13:38).

Chapter Six

THE CULT OF MARY

"For there is one God, and one mediator between God and men, the man Christ Jesus" *I Timothy* 2:5.

IT is difficult to deal with this heresy of Rome without seeming to detract from that blessed woman who was chosen of God to be the mother of our Lord. Far be it from me to speak one derogatory word concerning her, but the excesses of adulation indulged in by the Roman church demand an answer from Scripture. We are jealous for our Lord, "that in all things he might have the preeminence," and when we see a system which professes to be Christian setting up a rival to share the honor and the glory due to Christ alone, we must protest, however beautiful in character, exalted in office, or blessed in ministry that rival may be.

The cult of Mary is based on her sacred motherhood. But right here Rome makes its fundamental and fatal error. Instead of holding to the language of Scripture, Rome indulges a bit of syllogism to arrive at a false title for Mary. Mary is the mother of Jesus; Jesus is God; therefore Mary is the mother of God. There you have it, so simple, as they think, that none can dispute it. In their eyes, to question that Mary is the mother of God is to deny the deity of our Lord Jesus. Yet that attempt at logic on which such tremendous issues hang is, to use the language of law, a *non sequitur,* for it does not take all the factors into account. The deity and the preexistence of our Lord are inseparable. No creature, born in time, can be mother of that which is timeless. Mary is the mother of our Lord as man, not mother of our Lord as God. She is mother of the Man, Christ Jesus, not of God eternal. She is mother of the Man who is very God, not of God who became very man. The distinction is no mere juggling with words. It is the answer of true logic and true divinity to the blasphemous and idolatrous system which Rome builds on the unscriptural and untrue title, "Mother of God."

The Roman salutation addressed to Mary is, "Hail, Mary, full of grace," an echo of the angelic salutation at the time of the annunciation. The Greek word is the perfect passive participle, in the feminine gender, of a verb meaning "to show grace," and therefore means "a woman to whom grace has been shown," and who is therefore enjoying the blessing which grace bestowed. That is the straightforward, grammatical sense of the word. Rome, however, pours its own content of meaning into the term. The Rt. Rev. Msgr. Joseph Pohle, Ph. D., D. D. in his Mariology, says, "*kecharitomena* means a woman full of grace—endowed not merely with the extrinsic graces proper to her state of life, but with a full measure of sanctifying grace, which precedes the grace of vocation, strictly so called, by way of preparation and endowment."[1] Again, "the fullness of grace enjoyed by the Blessed Virgin Mary must be conceived as a superabundance of Interior Holiness."[2] This is a case of raising a term to the nth degree without warrant other than Rome's determination to exalt Mary beyond measure. The whole context indicates that the

---

1. Pohle-Preuss, *Mariology* (St. Louis, Mo., B. Herder Book Co., 1914), p. 25.
2. Ibid., p. 28.

grace bestowed on Mary was simply election to the high privilege of giving birth to our Lord. That God fitted the vessel is readily granted, but the text in question does not deal with the fitness, much less does it indicate what Rome intends by the "fullness of grace."

In the evangelical sense, grace and merit are never confused, but are mutually exclusive. Roman theology, however, constantly gets the two mixed up, and Mary is not spared. So we have this from Thomas Aquinas, one of the Doctors of the Roman Church: "By the *grace* bestowed upon her she *merited* that measure of purity and holiness which fitted her to be the mother of God."[3] That statement is contrary to the whole principle of grace. We merit nothing by grace, and grace bestows no merit. So long as we are objects of grace, we claim no merit. Grace is God's gift to the unmeriting, God's bounty to those who have no claim upon it. If Mary is *kecharitomena,* an object of God's grace, that is an end of all profession of merit.

Arising out of her divine motherhood, and in keeping with the "fullness of grace" which Rome attributes to her, Mary is said to have certain prerogatives. The first of these is the Immaculate Conception.

Here we come upon a dogma little understood by Protestants, many of whom think that the Immaculate Conception means that Mary conceived our Lord without sin. Indeed I have heard this term used as a synonym for the virgin birth of Christ. The dogma of the immaculate conception has nothing to do with the birth of Christ, but with the birth of Mary. It declares that Mary was conceived in her mother's womb entirely free from the taint of original sin.

---

3. Ibid., p. 27 (italics ours).

The Catholic Catechism, in answer to the question, "Has anyone been kept free from the stain of original sin?" declares, "The Blessed Virgin Mary alone was from the first instant of her conception, through the foreseen merits of Jesus Christ, by a unique privilege granted her by God, kept free from the stain of original sin; she is therefore said to have been 'conceived immaculate.' "[4] The word "immaculate" just means "without spot." The next question of the catechism is, "What does the Immaculate Conception of the Blessed Virgin Mary mean?"—and the answer, "The Immaculate Conception of the Blessed Virgin Mary means that from the first moment of her conception the Blessed Virgin Mary possessed justice and holiness—that is, sanctifying grace, even the fullness of grace, with the infused virtues and gifts of the Holy Ghost, and with integrity of nature."[5] Do you see how the snowball grows with rolling?

Let Pope Pius IX define the dogma still further for us: "We ... define that the ... Blessed Virgin Mary was in the first instant of her conception, by the singular grace and privilege of Almighty God, in virtue of the merits of Jesus Christ, the Saviour of the human race, preserved immune from all stain of original sin."[6]

Here is a little marvel of further exposition: "The dogma expressly says that our Lady owed her freedom from original sin entirely to the *redemptive merits* of her Divine Son."[7] Roman theology calls this "pre-redemption." According to this teaching, Mary was "redeemed" from the stain of sin *before she had it*. Now whatever that is, it is not redemption,

4. The Catholic Catechism, p. 81.
5. Ibid., p. 82.
6. Ibid., p. 280.
7. Pohle-Preuss, *Mariology*, p. 41 (italics ours).

neither pre- nor post-! No one is ever redeemed from a situation into which he has not come, but from a condition into which he has fallen. If Mary never had the stain of original sin, or any other sin, upon her, she was not redeemed, and the "redemptive merits" of her Divine Son never applied to her. To call it pre-redemption is to make mock of language and of common sense.

Rome is forced to two admissions in regard to the dogma of the immaculate conception. First, that it lacks scriptural evidence. "The dogma of the Immaculate Conception is not expressly enunciated in Sacred Scripture,"[8] says Pohle, supported by his editor Preuss; and again, when quoting two supporting Scriptures, he admits, "True, the exegetical argument from these texts, taken by itself, scarcely exceeds the limits of probability; but the lack of scriptural evidence can be abundantly supplied from the writings of the Fathers."[9] And Father S. J. Hunter complacently remarks that "this circumstance will have no weight against its acceptance, except with those who assume, without a scrap of reason, that the whole of the revelation given by God is contained in the inspired Books."[10] So the cat is out of the bag again: the real appeal of Rome is not to Scripture, but to tradition, and the teachings of the fathers. "To the law and to the testimony: if they speak not according to this word, it is because there is no light in them" (Isa. 8:20).

The second admission is that the doctrine of the immaculate conception was a subject of long controversy before it finally attained the status of a dogma of the church in the

8. Ibid., p. 42.
9. Ibid., p. 43.
10. Ibid., p. 42.

year 1854. Despite that fact, it is supported by the anathema of the church against all who refuse it.

The theological argument for the doctrine is summed up in the word "fitness." Three Latin words, after the order of Julius Caesar's famous trilogy, are used to present the argument: *potuit, decuit, fecit*. The meaning is: he could, he ought, he did. God was able to keep Mary free from the stain of original sin at her conception; it was fitting that He should do this for the vessel chosen to such holy use; therefore, He did it. As to God's ability we shall raise no question, at least on the biological side. There might be dispute from the moral angle. When, however, men take it on themselves to dictate what was fitting for God to do for Mary in view of her exalted task, they are becoming judges of God, and going beyond their rights; and when they make a dogma to the effect that God did so, on the bare ground that they decree it was the fit thing for Him to do, that is carrying presumption to great lengths. It is our privilege to admire the fitness of what God has manifestly done: it is not our privilege to legislate what God ought to do and make Him do it.

Mary's second prerogative is sinlessness. There are two aspects of this sinlessness. First, Mary had no inward stirrings, no motions of the flesh, in the direction of sin. She knew no concupiscence. There never were any risings in her heart to stir the slightest desire toward anything sinful. Then, as a result of this utter lack of any response to sin, she never committed a single, solitary sin of any kind, of omission or commission, in thought, word or deed. "The mother of God must have been endowed with a purity inferior only to that

of God Himself and His Christ."[11] Ephraim Syrus, addressing the virgin, says: "Mother of God ... all-pure, all-immacu-
late, all-stainless, all-undefiled, all-blameless, all-worthy of
praise, all-incorrupt; ... after the Trinity, mistress of all; after
the Paraclete, another consoler; and after the mediator, the
whole world's mediatrix; higher beyond compare than Cheru-
bim and Seraphim; ... fulness of the graces of the Trinity,
holding the second place after the Godhead."[12] The great
Council of Trent, at its sixth session, gave its decree regarding the sinlessness of Mary in this form: "If any one assert
that man, after he is once justified, is able to avoid throughout his lifetime all, even venial sin, except by a special divine
privilege, as the Church holds in regard to the Blessed Virgin, let him be anathema."[13]

It is not enough to declare Mary immaculate and sinless.
Rome goes yet farther and proclaims her impeccable—that is,
incapable of sin. Roman theologians draw some very fine
points of distinction between several types of impeccability.
The impeccability of God is metaphysical; the impeccability
of Christ is based on the hypostatic union (the union of deity
and humanity in one person); the impeccability of angels
arises from the beatific vision, their privilege of looking into
the face of God. The impeccability of Mary is of a different
order yet, but it does not seem to be clearly defined. This
impeccability does not only apply to her heavenly state, which
of course would be true of all glorified saints, but is pressed
for her entire earthly career, from birth to death.

The end is not yet. The sanctity of Mary is still further
augmented by the doctrine of the perpetual virginity. This

11. Ibid., p. 73.
12. Ibid., p. 74.
13. Ibid., p. 77.

dogma is stated in three parts: (1) Mary was a pure virgin before the birth of Christ; (2) Mary remained an inviolate virgin during parturition; (3) Mary remained a virgin after the birth of her Divine Son. There is a distinction drawn, you must observe, between the virgin conception and the virgin birth. When we speak of the virgin birth of our Lord, we mean what the Romanists refer to as the virgin conception, namely, that miracle by which Mary "was found with child of the Holy Ghost." When the Roman theologians speak of the virgin birth, they mean another miracle which they claim took place at the time of the birth of our Lord, not at the time of His conception: a miracle by which the birth occurred without affecting the virgin condition of the mother, so that she was as if she had never borne a child.

The point of controversy in the dogma, however, is the third part, which affirms that Mary remained a virgin all her life, despite her marriage with Joseph. According to Jerome, one of the doctors of the church, Joseph "was Mary's protector rather than her husband, and like her, had a celibate life."[14] According to Roman tradition, both Mary and Joseph had, in their early life, taken the vow of chastity, and when they were brought together in marriage they mutually agreed to sustain that vow. The question arises, what about the brethren of Christ? Rome's answer is that these brethren were not "brothers," but "kinsmen." The reading of Scripture would never have suggested that apart from the dogma of Rome. For with Rome it is not Scripture that moulds dogma, but dogma that determines the meaning of Scripture. While it does not affect our salvation whether James and Jude and Joses and Simon were Christ's half-brothers or cousins or

14. Ibid., p. 96.

great-uncles, we do protest against arbitrary readings of Holy Scripture for the buttressing of unscriptural dogmas.

Thomas Aquinas has given four reasons for holding the perpetual virginity of Mary: (1) the unique character of Christ as the only-begotten Son of God; (2) the honor and dignity of the Holy Ghost, who overshadowed her virginal womb; (3) the excellency of the title Deipara; and (4) the honor and chivalry of Joseph, who was commissioned to be the protector and guardian of his chaste spouse. It is noticeable that not one of these is an appeal to Scripture. They are imaginations, every one. A natural reading of Matthew's account will certainly suggest that after the birth of our Lord, Joseph and Mary lived a normal life. This whole dogma rests on a false Roman axiom that sanctity and wedlock are incompatible. Hence all their insistence on the celibacy of the priests, their glorification of virginity for their religious, and so on. It is one great blasphemy on the most hallowed of human relationships, God's own appointment for His creature man.

In a different category is the further prerogative of "bodily assumption." This doctrine declares that Mary was raised from the dead after three days, just as was our Lord, and like Him was received bodily up into heaven, only without the forty days between resurrection and ascension. Nobody knows when Mary died, nor where; nobody saw her rise from the dead, nor saw her alive after her resurrection; nobody saw her ascent into heaven. All this is so unlike the fully attested resurrection and ascension of our blessed Lord, yet it is held by Rome on "strictly dogmatic grounds."[15]

---

15. Ibid., p. 118.

Here is a paragraph out of a notable book, "The Life of the Blessed Virgin Mary":

"Vested with this wonderful glory, the holy Virgin arrived at the throne of the divinity, and the three divine Persons received her into their eternal and indissoluble embrace. She seemed as if absorbed within the three divine Persons, and as if submerged in that infinite ocean of the abyss of the Divinity; the saints heard these words of the Eternal Father: 'Our Daughter Mary has been elected and chosen by our eternal will as the only and singular one among all creatures, and she is also the first in our delights. She has never degenerated from her title of Daughter, which in the Divine Understanding has been given her from all eternity; therefore she has a right to our eternal kingdom, of which she is to be acknowledged and crowned the legitimate Sovereign and Queen.' "[16]

There can be only one issue of all this exaltation. One so endued with all grace, so immaculate in her conception, so sinless in her life, so impeccable in her nature, so glorified with special resurrection, so crowned in heaven, must be worshipped. But here again some fine distinctions are drawn. Rome has three kinds or degrees of worship: the worship of *dulia,* given to the saints; the worship of *latria,* offered to God alone; and in between these, the worship of *hyperdulia,* reserved for Mary, as being higher than the saints but inferior to God.

This technical distinction may placate the conscience of the Romanist in his breach of the cardinal law, quoted by our Lord Himself in His answer to Satan: "Thou shalt worship the Lord thy God, and him only shalt thou serve"

---

16. Mary of Jesus of Agreda, *The Life of the Blessed Virgin Mary* (abridged by De Caesare), p. 430.

(Matt. 4:10). As regards his worship of Mary, however, one is at a loss to discover any difference between the *hyperdulia* and the *latria*. In practice the distinction seems to be forgotten, till Mary receives more worship, so far as quantity is concerned, than God Himself; is glorified with titles and offices which belong to our Lord Jesus; and is offered such total consecration of body, soul, and spirit, as no one is entitled to, save God alone. The novenas are a splendid example of how Rome is really seeking to make this "the age of Mary."

Here is a prayer of St. Alphonsus, taken from the Little Flower Prayer Book:

"Most holy and immaculate Virgin! O my Mother! thou who art the Mother of my Lord, the Queen of the world, the advocate, hope, and refuge of sinners! I, the most wretched among them, now come to thee. I worship thee, great Queen, and give thee thanks for the many favors thou hast bestowed on me in the past; most of all do I thank thee for having saved me from hell, which I had so often deserved. I love thee, Lady most worthy of all love, and, by the love which I bear thee, I promise ever in the future to serve thee, and to do what in me lies to win others to thy love. In thee I put all my trust, all my hope of salvation. Receive me as thy servant, and cover me with the mantle of thy protection, thou who art the Mother of mercy! And since thou hast so much power with God, deliver me from all temptations, or at least obtain for me the grace ever to overcome them. From thee I ask a true love of Jesus Christ, and the grace of a happy death. O my Mother! by thy love for God, I beseech thee to be at all times my helper, but above all at the last moment of my life. Leave me not until you see me safe in heaven, there for endless ages to bless thee and sing thy praises. Amen."[17]

The saying of this prayer before an image or picture of the blessed virgin secures an indulgence of three hundred days!

Again, here is a typical act of consecration to Mary. I wonder if this is *dulia,* or *hyperdulia,* or unadulterated *latria?* —"My Queen! my Mother! I give myself entirely to thee; and to show my devotion to thee, I consecrate to thee this day my eyes, my ears, my mouth, my heart, my whole being, without reserve. Wherefore, good Mother, as I am thine own, keep me, guard me as thy property and possession."[18] This is to be said morning and evening for an indulgence of one hundred days!

One more example from Our Lady of Mt. Carmel Devotions. Mary speaks: "I am the Help of Christians. Wilt thou, my dear child, obey the Precepts of the Holy Catholic Church, and call upon me in thy necessities? If thou wilt do so, I will assist thee, my dear child, and assure thee, with a heart truly maternal, that I will plead for thee in time of danger, *and will avert from thee all the anger and indignation of my Divine Son.*"[19] Is Mary more merciful than our Lord who for our salvation shed His own precious blood? Is Mary more understanding, more compassionate than our great High Priest who stooped to temptation and humiliation, and suffering, and death, all to fit Himself to be our sole representative? Such blasphemy is sufficient to condemn the whole system.

---

17. The Little Flower Prayer Book, p. 298.
18. Ibid., p. 91.
19. Ibid., p. 234 (italics ours).

Titles are multiplied upon Mary. They fall into four divisions: the mother titles, the queen titles, the virgin titles, and the mystical titles. Among the mystical titles are: "Seat of Wisdom, Tower of David, Ark of the Covenant, Gate of Heaven, Morning Star, Refuge of Sinners, our Hope and our Life." The bestowal of such titles is a wresting of glory from the brow of our Lord, to whom alone are they due.

The offices ascribed to Mary are likewise a usurpation of the place of Christ. She is the second Eve, she is the advocate, she is the mediatrix, she is the co-redemptrix. Rome teaches: "even as Eve brought in sin and death, so Mary brings in obedience and life, and as we owe all our miseries to Eve, so we owe all of the blessings of salvation to Mary." Scripture teaches: "as in Adam all die, even so in Christ shall all be made alive" (I Cor. 15:22)—"for as by the one man's disobedience many were made sinners, so by the obedience of one (masc.) shall many be made righteous" (Rom. 5:19). Who is right, Rome or Paul? The teaching of Scripture is equally opposed to the other mediatorial offices ascribed to Mary. "There is one God, and one mediator between God and men, the man Christ Jesus" (I Tim. 2:5).

I have refrained from dealing with the extravagances of many of the devotees of Mary, but have confined myself to a demonstration of the general teaching of the church of Rome. Surely enough has been said to show how foreign is all this Mariolatry to the teachings of Scripture, how damaging it is to the unique glories of Christ our Lord, and how damning it must all be to the souls who engage in it. Yet, it is as a spell cast upon so many millions whose eyes are holden by it. May the Lord send a new awakening to deliver many who are bound!

Chapter Seven

ROME'S WAY OF SALVATION

"For by grace are ye saved through faith; and that not of yourselves: it is the gift of God: Not of works, lest any man should boast" *Ephesians* 2:8, 9.

ROME'S way of salvation is the sacramental way, which differs vastly from the evangelical way. By the sacramental way we mean that salvation is ministered through ordinances: by the evangelical way we mean that salvation is received by faith at the hearing of the gospel.

The church of Rome holds that there are seven sacraments, five of which minister saving grace: baptism, confirmation, the eucharist, penance, and extreme unction. The other two are matrimony and ordination. Only the sacraments of salvation concern us at the moment.

The classic Roman definition of a sacrament is that given by Augustine: "A Sacrament is a sign of a sacred thing." If it stopped there we should be in perfect agreement. But in further explanation of the nature of a sacrament, the Catechism of the Council of Trent for Parish Priests, perhaps the most authoritative statement of Roman doctrine and practice in existence, declares, "It is a sensible object which possesses, by divine institution, the power not only of signifying, but also of accomplishing holiness and righteousness."[1] Again,

---

1. *Catechism of the Council of Trent for Parish Priests* (Trans. by McHugh and Callan, Second Revised Edition, 1937), p. 146.

"No one can doubt that the Sacraments are among the means of attaining righteousness and salvation."[2]

The *first* sacrament is baptism. Let the Catholic Catechism define it for us: "The sacrament of baptism is a sacrament of cleansing instituted by Jesus Christ; by it the person baptized is made a member of the true church of Jesus Christ, obtains remission of original sin and of all actual sins if he has committed any, with all the punishment due to them, and becomes capable of receiving the other sacraments."[3]

Perhaps we should pause to explain original sin. When we use that term we are not bringing up the question of the particular nature of the first sin committed by Adam and Eve. By the term "original sin" we signify that every one of us comes into the world with the taint of sin upon us, inherited from our first father, Adam. Some hold that we are actually guilty of that sin of Adam, since we were all in Adam when he sinned. Others stress merely the sinful nature with which we are born, and by which we are ready to resist God from birth. You will remember that, according to the teaching of Rome, Mary, the mother of our Lord, was miraculously exempted from this stain of original sin. That is what is meant by the immaculate conception. Whatever we think of that dogma, we had better all admit that the rest of us were born with the stain of original sin.

For that part of our lost condition baptism is the cure offered by Rome. "Baptism," says Cardinal Gibbons, "is the essential means established for washing away the stain of original sin."[4] Using baptism as an example of the efficacy

---

2. Ibid., p. 143.
3. *The Catholic Catechism*, p. 157.
4. *The Faith of Our Fathers*, p. 268.

of sacraments in general, the Catechism of the Council of Trent affirms: "Baptism, for instance, which is administered by external ablution, accompanied with certain solemn words, signifies that by the power of the Holy Ghost all stain and defilement of sin is inwardly washed away, and that the soul is enriched and adorned with the admirable gift of heavenly justification; while, at the same time, the bodily washing, as we shall hereafter explain in its proper place, accomplishes in the soul that which it signifies."[5] Now if it had stopped at the word "justification," we Protestants would have rejoiced in such a splendid statement. The power of the water to cleanse interiorly was imparted to it at the baptism of our Lord, as Augustine says: "From the moment that Christ is immersed in water, water washes away all sins. . . . The Lord is baptized, not because He had need to be cleansed, but in order that, by the contact of His pure flesh, He might purify the waters and impart to them the power of cleansing."[6]

Baptism, according to this same supreme authority, has six effects:

(1) "Such is the admirable efficacy of this sacrament that it remits original sin and actual guilt."

(2) "In baptism not only is sin forgiven, but with it all the punishment due to sin is mercifully remitted by God." (This includes the punishment due to original sin in the next world.)

(3) The grace of regeneration, by which we "are also enriched with invaluable goods and blessings."

(4) "This grace is accompanied by a most splendid train

---

5. *Catechism of the Council of Trent*, p. 144.
6. Ibid., p. 170.

of all virtues, which are divinely infused into the soul along with grace."

(5) "By baptism, moreover, we are sealed with a character that can never be effaced from the soul."

(6) "It opens to us the portals of heaven which sin has closed against us."[7]

Baptism is the one all-essential sacrament, without which there is no salvation. "Unless they are regenerated to God through the grace of baptism, be their parents Christians or infidels, they are born to eternal misery and destruction."[8] This involves the need of baptizing infants, lest they should die before the age of reason and be lost. The Catechism of the Council of Trent is strangely silent on the end of babes who die without baptism, but the Catechism of Cardinal Gasparri has this: "The souls of those who die without baptism but in a state of original sin only, lack the beatific vision of God, but do not suffer other penalties such as are reserved for personal sins."[9] That doubtless refers to new-born babes. Cardinal Gibbons softens the situation by the following explanation: "It is proper here to state briefly what the Church actually teaches regarding the future state of unbaptized infants. Though the Church, in obedience to God's Word, declares that unbaptized infants are excluded from the kingdom of heaven, it should not hence be concluded that they are consigned to the place of the reprobate. None are condemned to the torments of the damned but such as merit divine vengeance by their personal sins. All that the Church holds on this point is that unregenerate children are deprived of the

7. Ibid., p. 183 seq.
8. *Catechism of the Council of Trent*, p. 177.
9. *The Catholic Catechism*, p. 160.

beatific vision, or the possession of God, which constitutes the essential happiness of the blessed. Now, between the supreme bliss of heaven and the torments of the reprobate, there is a very wide margin. All admit that the condition of unbaptized infants is better than non-existence. There are some Catholic writers of distinction who even assert that unbaptized infants enjoy a certain degree of natural beatitude—that is, a happiness which is based on the natural knowledge and love of God."[10]

Two exceptions to the universal requirement of baptism are allowed. If one has embraced the faith, and is a catechumen, preparing for baptism, but dies suddenly before receiving the rite, his intention is accepted for the deed. That is called the "Baptism of Desire." The classic case cited is the Emperor Valentinian, whose death St. Ambrose lamented, saying, "I lost him whom I was about to regenerate, but he did not lose the grace he sought for." The other case of dispensation is martyrdom, called the "Baptism of Blood," which is accepted as more than equivalent to the sacrament.

The *second* sacrament is confirmation. In this rite a bishop receives the person who has been baptized and instructed, lays his hands on him, makes the sign of the cross with the holy chrism made of olive oil and balsam, and slaps him on the cheek. While he is applying the oil the bishop says: "I sign thee with the sign of the cross, and I confirm thee with the chrism of salvation, in the name of the Father, and of the Son, and of the Holy Ghost." The imposition of hands follows apostolic custom, and is for the receiving of the Holy Spirit. The slap on the cheek is to signify that a Christian must endure suffering for Christ.

---

10. *The Faith of our Fathers*, p. 273.

While confirmation is not held as "absolutely necessary for salvation" as is baptism, yet, according to the catechism, "it is wrong to neglect it, because it is a means for obtaining salvation more easily and fully."[11]

Now we believe that instruction in the Word and experience of God keep on confirming the believing soul, but confirmation to the Romanist is a sacramental rite, bestowing grace. "Those who have been made Christians by baptism, still have in some sort the tenderness and softness, as it were, of new-born infants, and afterwards become, by means of the Sacrament of chrism, stronger to resist the assaults of the world, the flesh and the devil, while their minds are fully confirmed in faith to confess and glorify the name of our Lord Jesus Christ."[12] In a word, the sacrament of confirmation is regarded as doing for those who receive it what Pentecost did for the original group of disciples when the Holy Spirit came upon them. "For by this Sacrament the Holy Spirit infuses Himself into the souls of the faithful, and increases in them strength and fortitude to enable them, in the spiritual contest, to fight manfully and to resist their most wicked foes."[13] The efficacy of the rite is stated by St. Cyril of Jerusalem in his Catecheses XXI, 3, in these words: "Take care not to regard this ointment as something empty and meaningless. For just as the Eucharistic bread is, after the invocation of the Holy Spirit, no longer ordinary bread but the Body of Christ, so too is this ointment no longer, after the invocation, a bare—or as some would prefer to say—an ordinary ointment, it is the treasure-chamber of Christ and

11. *The Catholic Catechism*, p. 163.
12. *Catechism of the Council of Trent*, p. 209.
13. Ibid., p. 211

of the Holy Spirit, made efficacious by the presence of His Godhead."

The Scripture commonly used in exposition of the sacrament is II Corinthians 1:21, on which Cardinal Gibbons comments: " 'He that confirmeth us with you in Christ, and that hath anointed us, is God; who also hath sealed us and given the pledge of the Spirit in our hearts.' God *confirmeth* us in faith; He hath *anointed* us by spiritual unction, typified by the sacred chrism which is marked on our foreheads. He hath *sealed* us by the indelible character stamped on our souls, which is indicated by the sign of the cross impressed on us. He hath given the *pledge* of the Holy Ghost in our hearts, by the testimony of a good conscience, as an earnest of future glory. The Bishop performs the external unction, but God, 'who worketh all in all,' sanctifies the soul by His secret operation."[14]

The *third* sacrament is the eucharist, so closely linked with the sacrifice of the mass. In this sacrament the faithful receive the body and blood, along with the soul and divinity, of the Lord. Having already given some attention to this, we shall be content now to mention the grace which is claimed to be derived from this sacrament. "The Holy Eucharist is most efficacious toward the attainment of eternal glory,"[15] says the Trent Catechism. It remits venial (that is, lesser) sins, it strengthens against temptation, it invigorates and nourishes the soul. For all the urgency of baptism, this is still greater, for in this sacrament alone Christ gives Himself to the communicant, and He being the fountain and source of all graces,

---

14. *The Faith of our Fathers*, p. 281.
15. *Catechism of the Council of Trent*, p. 244.

all graces are multiplied by the sacrament of the body and blood.

Parish priests are exhorted to expound the benefits of the eucharist from the sixth chapter of John's Gospel. There three things are stated regarding the receiving of the body and blood of the Lord. First, he has no life who does not partake of them. Second, he has eternal life who does, and will be raised up in the resurrection of the just. Third, eating and drinking of the body and blood of Christ is the way to realize the mutual indwelling of Christ and the believer. If, then, it is alone in the sacrament that we eat His flesh and drink His blood, then the sacrament of the eucharist is essential to eternal life, to the resurrection, and to Christ's indwelling presence.

The *fourth* sacrament is penance. As we have seen, the sacrament of baptism remits original sin and actual sin up to that time, including all punishment. So at baptism one is in a perfect state of grace. The sacraments of confirmation and the eucharist strengthen and fortify against sin, and the latter remits venial sins. But despite all that, sins are most likely to creep in, even mortal sins, sins of the major type, and they have to be dealt with. It is important to observe that mortal sin damns the soul even of the baptized, so that one who has committed mortal sin is as much lost as if he had never been baptized. The Council of Trent, in its sixth and fourteenth session, declared: "For those who fall into sin after Baptism the Sacrament of Penance is as neccesary to salvation as is Baptism for those who have not been already baptized."[16] And the compilers of the catechism ordered by the same council add: "As he who suffers shipwreck has no

---

16. Ibid., p. 261.

hope of safety, unless, perchance, he seize on some plank from the wreck, so he that suffers the shipwreck of baptismal innocence, unless he cling to the saving plank of Penance, has doubtless lost all hope of salvation."

Because mortal sin brings eternal punishment, some way of remission must be found for restoring the reconciliation and the state of grace. The sacrament of penance is the way proposed. In it the sinner comes to the priest as confessor, and three things are required of him—contrition, confession, and satisfaction. The contrition demanded is that state of heart which we generally term repentance. Certainly no fault can be found with that. Then full confession must be made to the priest in the secrecy of the confessional. Direct access to Christ as great High Priest is not permitted, since the power of the keys, for binding and loosing, was given to the priesthood in the person of Peter. The satisfaction is the work of penance imposed by the priest, with the twofold purpose of working off the temporal punishment for the sins committed and fortifying the soul against a repetition of the sins. The priest on his part grants absolution for the sin committed, so remitting the eternal punishment and restoring the soul to favour with God. The priest, it is to be noted, does not merely pronounce the absolution, but bestows it. "Unlike the priests of the Old Law who merely declared the leper cleansed from his leprosy, the power now given to the priests of the New Law is not limited to declaring the sinner absolved from his sins, but, as a minister of God, he truly absolves from sin."[17] Moreover, this is the only way of salvation for those who have sinned after baptism. "Returning now to the Sacrament, it is so much the special province of Penance," says

17. Ibid., p. 269.

the catechism, "to remit sins that it is impossible to obtain or even to hope for remission of sins by any other means."[18]

Let the Catholic Catechism teach us the effects of the sacrament of penance:

(1) "his sin and its eternal punishment, also—at least partially—the debt of temporal punishment due to sin, are remitted;

(2) "his merits which were annulled by his mortal sins, revive—that is, they regain the efficacy which, before his falling into mortal sin, they had for winning him eternal life;

(3) "a special grace is given for avoiding sin in the future."[19]

In regard to the last mentioned effect, Cardinal Gibbons calls the confessional (which in this case really stands for the entire sacrament) "the most powerful lever ever erected by a merciful God for raising men from the mire of sin."

The *fifth* sacrament is extreme unction. The baptized, confirmed, communicated, and confessed Catholic dies like the rest of us, and the Church has provided a sacrament for his last moments. Extreme unction is now given. In this sacrament the priest anoints the eyes, ears, mouth, nose, head, and feet of the dying one, saying, "Through this holy unction and His most tender mercy, may the Lord pardon thee whatever faults thou hast committed by sight, hearing, smell, taste, touch, and walking," or some other formula according to the special order to which the priest belongs. By this

18. Ibid., p. 271
19. *The Catholic Catechism*, p. 184.

sacrament, the vestiges of sin are removed, strength is imparted to resist the last temptations, courage is given for the last agony of death, while in some cases the sick one recovers. "For this 'thing' is the grace of the Holy Spirit, whose unction blots out any sins if any yet remain to be expiated, as also the remains of sin; it also relieves and confirms the soul of the sick man by arousing in him a great confidence in the Divine mercy, so that the sick person is consoled and thus bears more readily the inconveniences and discomforts of his sickness; he also resists more easily the assaults of the devil 'lying in wait for his heel,' and sometimes, when it is expedient for the salvation of his soul, he recovers his bodily health."[20]

The Scripture on which this sacrament is based is James 5:14, 15. Where physically possible, the sick person is expected to make confession, or at least an act of contrition. I suggest only in passing that Rome has turned a healing rite into a dying sacrament.

So much for the sacraments: but the end is not yet. After the regeneration of baptism, the fortification of confirmation, the nourishment of the mass, the remission of penance, and the final ordering of extreme unction, salvation is not yet attained. For even if all mortal sins have been confessed and remitted with their eternal punishment, there still remains the question of temporal punishment, part of which may have been endured in this world, both by providences of God and acts of satisfaction and voluntary penances, but the remainder of which waits for accounting in the life beyond. The place appointed for this temporal punishment is purgatory.

---

20. Ibid., p. 415.

It must be understood that the sins punished in purgatory have already been remitted, but satisfaction is yet required. David's suffering in the death of his illegitimate child born of Uriah's wife, and Miriam's week of isolation for leprosy after both had been forgiven their sins are cited as proofs of temporal punishment after the remission of sin.

Double pain is endured in purgatory—the pain of loss and the pain of sense: "they are, that is, deprived for a time of the beatific vision of God and they suffer other grave pains."[21] The length and intensity of the pains of purgatory depend on the amount of punishment due. Nobody in this world can ever tell you whether or not your loved one is yet out of purgatory.

But there is the possibility of shortening and alleviating the pains of purgatory. The two means are indulgences and suffrages. The more indulgences a person can obtain before death the shorter and easier will be his detention in purgatory.

What are indulgences? First of all, they are not, as many think, permissions to sin. "By an indulgence we mean the remission by God of the temporal punishment due to sins whose guilt has already been forgiven; such forgiveness the Church grants apart from the sacrament of penance."[22]

The basis of indulgences is the superabundant satisfaction of the blood of Christ with the added satisfaction of the Virgin Mary and the saints. This is called the spiritual treasury of the Church. St. Thomas Aquinas says of it: "All this treasure is at the dispensation of the chief rulers of the Church, inasmuch as our Lord gave the Keys of the Church

21. Ibid., p. 457.
22. Ibid., p. 185.

to Peter. When then the utility or necessity of the Church requires it, the chief ruler of the Church can draw from this infinite store of merits to communicate to any one who through charity is a member of the Church, as much as he deems to be opportune, whether it be such as will suffice for the total remission of his punishment, or up to a certain portion of the whole: in such wise, namely, that the Passion of Christ (through whom alone the merits of the others have efficacy) and the other saints may be imparted to him just as if he himself had suffered what was necessary for the remission of his sin—as happens when one person satisfies for another."

There are various means of securing indulgences, but chiefly by works of devotion as reading the Scriptures, offering certain prayers, attending to religious exercises, giving time to teaching or learning the catechism, and a thousand other ways. The indulgences are usually authorized by the Pope.

The church used to impose canonical punishment, and of course had the right to revoke any or part of the penalty imposed. The canonical punishments are discontinued, but the dispensation of indulgences continues. "An Indulgence, for instance, of forty days remits, before God, so much of the temporal punishment as would have been expiated in the primitive Church by a canonical penance of forty days."[23] Thus, the more indulgences one can obtain, the easier and shorter the time in purgatory.

After one has gone to purgatory, something can still be done by way of alleviation. Those who remain on earth can pray for him, have masses said for him, and apply indulgences

---

23. *The Faith of our Fathers*, p. 378.

to him by way of suffrage. "Unless the contrary is stated we can apply the Indulgences we gain to the souls detained in Purgatory when such Indulgences have been granted by the Roman Pontiff."[24] This last, however, is not very satisfactory, according to Dr. O'Brien, for we cannot be sure that the one to whom we apply them will receive the benefit. "There is an important difference in the application of indulgences to the living and to the dead. The living are subjects of the Church's immediate jurisdiction; the deceased are not. To the former she grants an indulgence as an exercise of her judiciary authority. To the latter she makes an indulgence available by way of suffrage. That is, she petitions God, under whose sole jurisdiction the deceased are, to accept the works of satisfaction and in consideration thereof to mitigate the sufferings of the souls in purgatory. Can we say, therefore, that an indulgence gained by the living for any individual in purgatory will be applied with infallible certainty to that particular soul? While we piously believe that the individual soul will be benefited to some degree, we cannot say with certainty that it will be applied in its entirety to that particular soul. That lies within the jurisdiction of Almighty God, and we rest content with the knowledge that the case is in the hands of a Father Who is both infinitely just and infinitely merciful."[25]

Beloved, if elaboration could secure salvation and the assurance of it, surely salvation and the assurance of it would be found in Rome, with such an elaborate system of salvation as I have tried to present to you briefly; but, ask a Catholic—a good Catholic, a religious among the Catholics, ask

---

24. *The Catholic Catechism,* p. 186.
25. *The Faith of Millions,* p. 209.

him, ask her—"Are you saved?" and the best answer you will get is this: "Nobody can know that he is saved until after he dies."

To what avail is it all?—your regenerating baptism, your establishing confirmation, your nourishing eucharist, your remitting penance, your last exercise of extreme unction, your suffering in purgatory, your scrambling to get indulgences, and your glowing prayers for your friends who have gone. To what avail is it all if it gives not assurance? The gospel of Jesus Christ offers salvation with assurance! The gospel of Jesus Christ says, "God so loved the world, that he gave his only begotten Son, that whosoever believeth in him should not perish, but have everlasting life" (John 3:16). Rome has inserted between the "believing" and the "having eternal life," the sacrament of baptism, the sacrament of confirmation, the sacrament of the eucharist, the sacrament of penance, the sacrament of extreme unction, indulgences, and purgatory, and then you do not arrive at having eternal life! The best you can arrive at is "hoping to be saved."

The gospel of Jesus Christ says, "The wages of sin is death; but the gift of God is eternal life through Jesus Christ our Lord" (Rom. 6:23). But Rome puts between the believing sinner and that free gift, the exercise of the sacraments, the "heaping up" of merits, the multiplying of good works. "The gift of God is eternal life through Jesus Christ our Lord," but Rome steps in between the sinner and Jesus Christ our Lord saying, "Yes, it comes through Him, but you cannot receive it, save by way of the Church, the Priest, the Sacraments, and the rest of it!"

So every one of our great gospel passages is taken up by Rome, drained of its immediacy, its assurance, its freeness, and subjected to the inventions and corruptions of a sacramentarianism which makes the grace of God of no effect by its system of merits, and gives the finished work of Christ a dubious place in the background of the salvation picture, while the works of men fill the canvas. How, then, shall we counteract Rome's false counsel, "Go to the Church; go to the priest; go to Mary; go to Joseph; go to the sacraments?" We must do this by ringing out our Lord's blessed invitation, "Come unto me, all ye that labor and are heavy laden, and I will give you rest" (Matt. 11:28), and His equally blessed assurance, "Him that cometh to me I will in no wise cast out" (John 6:37).

Chapter Eight

ROME IN HISTORY

"Ye shall know them by their fruits" *Matthew* 7:16.

AND he said unto them, When I sent you without purse, and scrip, and shoes, lacked ye any thing? And they said, Nothing. Then said he unto them, But now, he that hath a purse, let him take it, and likewise his scrip: and he that hath no sword, let him sell his garment, and buy one. . . And they said, Lord, behold, here are two swords. And he said unto them, It is enough" (Luke 22:35, 36, 38). Such is the record of the evangelist.

Now hear the interpretation of Pope Boniface VIII: "There is one fold and one shepherd. The authority of that shepherd includes the two swords,—the spiritual and the temporal. So much are we taught by the words of the evangelist, 'Behold, here are two swords,' namely, in the Church. The Lord did not reply, 'It is too much,' but, 'It is enough.' Certainly he did not deny to Peter the temporal sword: he only commanded him to return it into its scabbard. Both, therefore, belong to the jurisdiction of the Church,—the spiritual sword and the secular. The one is to be wielded *for* the Church, the other *by* the Church; the one is the sword of the priest, the other is in the hand of the monarch, but at the command and sufferance of the priest. It behoves the one sword to be under the other, the temporal authority to be subject to the spiritual power."[1]

---

1. Corpus Juris Canonici, 1631.

Here is an excellent sample of Roman hermeneutics! But more to the point, it is no idle dream; it is a basic principle of the papacy. The claim to temporal power has not always been uttered so unequivocally, for expediency has, at times, required a softening of that note, but so long as the crown of the pope is a tiara, the claim of universal dominion persists.

Whenever the papacy has had sufficient power to press its claims, it has done so to the uttermost; kings, emperors, and rulers being forced to bow to the will of the Roman priest. Direct interference in the political affairs of the nations has been unblushingly practiced, and resistance met with the thunders of excommunication and interdict.

The thirteenth century marked the peak of papal power, when all Europe trembled at the blasts of the Roman trumpet. When England was tottering under the burden of taxes extorted by King John to make up for the losses of his French possessions, Pope Innocent III demanded English money to finance his war against the Hohenstaufens on the continent. Then, when the same King John resisted the pope on the question of appointment to the see of Canterbury, the pope not only pronounced excommunication and interdict, but persuaded King Philip of France to prepare an invasion of England. Once more, when the barons of England resisted the tyranny of John and secured the first great step toward constitutional monarchy in the Magna Charta, the pope issued a bull of annulment. The papacy has resisted the advance of freedom from the beginning

Pope Pius VI united practice with the enunciation of principle. In his bull against Queen Elizabeth of England, published in 1570, he says: "He who reigneth on high, to whom is given all power in heaven and in earth, hath committed the one holy Catholic Church, out of which there is no salvation, to one alone upon earth, that is, to Peter, the prince of apostles, and to the Roman Pontiff, the successor of Peter, to be governed with a plenitude of power. This one he hath constituted prince over all nations, that he may pluck up, overthrow, disperse, destroy, plant, and rear." On the basis of that claim comes the act of deposition: "We deprive the Queen of her pretended right to the kingdom, and of all dominion, dignity, and privilege whatsoever; and absolve all the nobles, subjects, and people of the kingdom, and whoever else have sworn to her, from their oath, and all duty whatsoever in regard of dominion, fidelity, and obedience."[2]

These are just a few of many examples that might be cited of direct papal interference in the affairs of England. The nations of continental Europe could furnish a long catalogue of similar instances in their own history. Time was that kings held their lands as fiefs of the Roman overlord. The wielding of the temporal sword was, of course, to a distinctly spiritual end, namely, the complete sovereignty of the papacy!

Time came when popes could no longer ride roughshod over the nations. The measure of the papacy's inability to enforce its will has been the measure in which it has innocently denied intention to do so, while only changing the means of seeking its end. The weapon of intrigue may be less direct, but it is very effectual when skillfully handled. The papacy has had long experience of the tool, and has become a master-craftsman in its use. In the very year which witnessed the loss of the temporal power of the Vatican, 1870, the claims of the papacy were revived, or at least re-stated,

2. N.B. Queen Elizabeth kept on reigning!

in the Vatican decrees. Referring to these, the great Gladstone wrote, "The claims of Gregory VII, of Innocent III, and of Boniface VIII have been disinterred in the nineteenth century, like hideous mummies picked out of Egyptian sarcophagi," but added that this revival was not "in the interests of archaeology, or without a definite and practical aim."[3] Protestant and democratic nations have had good reason to acknowledge the truth of Gladstone's statement.

It is of more than passing interest that the writer of a splendid life of John Huss[4] should later be the very one to restore the temporal power of the papacy and have his ravaging of Ethiopia given the papal benediction as a blessed crusade. Rome's championship of fascism is notorious.

Franco's rise to power in Spain was not by the will of the people, who were having their first taste of freedom under the new democracy, but by the will of the papacy, assisted by "volunteer" divisions from Italy and Germany. John Gunther has a frontispiece map of Europe in his *Inside Europe*. Spain is marked as No. 24, and the accompanying note says:

"24 Spain. Here a Fascist coup d'etat plunged a nation into bloody civil war. Here a Left Republic tried to bring 25,000,000 Spaniards to daylight. *Here the church, the feudal aristocracy, the predatory generals, turned the clock back.* Here Germans and Italians intervened to help General Franco with almost 100,000 troops."

In the body of his book, dealing with the Spanish Civil War, Gunther says:

"On the rebel or insurgent side (called the 'Nationalists' in pro-Franco newspapers) were, speaking broadly, the offi-

3. Morley's *Life of Gladstone*, Vol. 2 (London: Edward Lloyd, 1908), p. 92.
4. Benito Mussolini, *John Hus*, translated by Clifford Parker (Grand Rapids: Zondervan, 1929).

cer class, the feudal aristocracy, *the bulk of the politically minded Roman Catholics,* the monarchists, the Carlists from Navarre, the Falangistas or Fascists, the army officers, some of the industrialists, and part of the national police force or Civil Guard. Their rank-and-file fighting force contained Germans, Italians, Moorish troops from Spanish Morocco and the Riff, and the Spanish Foreign Legion— *in a word, comparatively few authentic Spaniards except the Carlists and Falangistas."*[5]

The prominence of the "church" in this reactionary and Fascist movement is noted by this keen and by no means prejudiced observer.

Roman Catholic Ireland has played badly in both world wars. In the war of 1914-18 Michael Collins, a Roman Catholic priest, and Sir Roger Casement were leaders in the rebellion. Sir Roger was later executed as a traitor. It was not, however, till years later that the hand of the "church" was revealed. On May 26, 1933, *The Irish Press* carried an editorial containing the following:

"Today Ireland learns for the first time one of the most moving and glorious stories in connection with the Easter Week Rising. Before it took place Pope Benedict XV received a Mission from the Irish Volunteer Executive in the person of George Noble, Count Plunkett. The Count had an audience for two hours with His Holiness, and disclosed to him the decision to rise and the date of the insurrection, and received from him his Apostolic Benediction on the men who were facing death for Ireland's liberty."[6]

In World War II Eire won the distinction of being the

---

5. John Gunther, *Inside Europe*, 1938 edition (New York: Harper & Bros. Copyright 1933, 1934, 1935, 1936, 1937, 1938, Reprinted by permission), p. 166.
6. Quoted in *The Gospel Witness*, Toronto; Jan. 2, 1941.

only part of the British Empire to stand aloof, even refusing the use of her ports in the critical Battle of the Atlantic. For her magnificent contribution the Axis powers assured her of support if she were attacked by Britain! The guarantee was given in an Italian broadcast which said: "Should the Irish people be forced to defend themselves against British agression, they can be assured of the full and wholehearted help of the Axis powers. Beside this military help the whole Catholic world would be on their side."[7] The last sentence of the broadcast is interesting for our present subject.

The same political genius is at work in Roman Catholic Quebec, and in both world wars the same powers have opposed and undermined the Canadian effort. The Global War of the '40's found the Roman Catholic politicians standing against full participation. Indeed the famous (or infamous) Sirois Report declared that it was "an extraordinary concession to Canadian unity on the part of French Canada"[8] to submit to any participation in the European War. When the Mobilization Law of 1940 was passed, it actually restricted the powers of the government to draft men for overseas duty, and Roman Catholic Quebec claimed the laurels for that restriction. Premier Godbout of Quebec, in a speech delivered at Plessisville, Quebec, said in this regard: "We are a minority in this country. The English who arrived here after us are more attached to England than we are, and that is perfectly understandable. They would have desired to have

---

7. *The Globe and Mail*, Toronto; Dec. 28, 1940.
8. "Le Canada français a subi, dans le silence et l'obéissance à l'authorité dûment constituée, le principe de la participation à la guerre d' Europe. M. Mackenzie King sera le premier à admettre que c'était là, une concession extraordinaire à l'unité canadienne, de la part du Canada français."

conscription for overseas service established. But a little hand-
ful of French Canadians, led by Mr. Ernest Lapointe, dictated
their will to the country."[9]

The immediate restoration of the forfeited privileges of
the Roman Church in Vichy France is sufficient to indicate
what were the influences behind the fall of France and the
whole collaboration movement. A dispatch from Vatican City
on July 15, 1940, declared: "Pope Pius XII was said to be convinced that Marshal Pétain and Vice-Premier Pierre Laval
will work for the reconstruction of French national life *in
line with policies which will meet with approval of the
church*."[10] He was not mistaken, for the *Daily Telegraph* of
London was able to carry this on September 12 of the same
year: "Messages from Vichy reveal that France ended a 36-
year rift between Church and State when the Vichy government formally repealed a law of 1904, thus abrogating a
series of discriminatory measures then designed to restrict
the influence of the Catholic Church in the field of education. . . A new decree issued restores the spirit of the con-
cordat signed between Napoleon Bonaparte and Pope Pius
VII, permitting Jesuits to teach in Catholic educational institutions and allowing convents to reopen officially."

High ecclesiastics were both open and ardent in their
espousal of the collaboration programme. A Roman Catholic,
writing of Cardinal Baudrillart, says of him: "He brought to
the government of Marshal Pétain an adherence worth an

9. "Nous sommes une minorité en ce pays. Les Anglais qui sont arrivés
ici, après nous, sont plus attachés que nous à l'Angleterre et cela se
comprend parfaitement. Ils auraient voulu que la conscription fût
établie pour service outre-mer. Mais une petite poignée de Canadiens
français, conduite par M. Ernest Lapointe, a dicté ses volontés au pays."
10. Emphasis ours. J. C. M.

army. Then he became, and remained until his death, one of the leaders of collaboration with the Nazis. He was lavish in his encouragements to the 'French legionnaires' who, having donned the German uniform and sworn allegiance to Hitler, went to Russia to fight and die in order to make definitive the victory of the Nazis and the enslavement of the French people."[11]

So much for Rome in the political sphere. In the social sphere the record is no better.

Lord Macaulay was no rabid foe of the Church of Rome. He is generous in his praise where it can be given. Yet, after evaluating the work of the hierarchy in the Middle Ages, he has this to say:

"During the last three centuries, to stunt the growth of the human mind has been her chief object. Throughout Christendom, whatever advance has been made in knowledge, in freedom, in wealth, and in the arts of life, has been made in spite of her, and has everywhere been in inverse proportion to her power. The loveliest and most fertile provinces of Europe have, under her rule, been sunk in poverty, in political servitude, and in intellectual torpor; while Protestant countries, once proverbial for sterility and barbarism, have been turned, by skill and industry, into gardens, and can boast of a long list of heroes and statesmen, philosophers, and poets. Whoever, knowing what Italy and Scotland naturally are, and what, four hundred years ago, they actually were, shall now compare the country round Rome with the country round Edinburgh, will be able to form some judgment as to the tendency of Papal domination. The descent of Spain, once

11. Yves R. Simon, *"The March of Liberation,"* p. 41. Quoted in *The Converted Catholic,* November, 1944, p. 247

the first among monarchies, to the lowest depths of degrada-
tion, the elevation of Holland, in spite of many natural dis-
advantages, to a position such as no commonwealth so small
has ever reached, teach the same lesson. Whoever passes in
Germany from a Roman Catholic to a Protestant principality,
in Switzerland from a Roman Catholic to a Protestant canton,
in Ireland from a Roman Catholic to a Protestant county,
finds that he has passed from a lower to a higher grade of
civilization. On the other side of the Atlantic the same law
prevails. The Protestants of the United States have left far
behind them the Roman Catholics of Mexico, Peru, and
Brazil. The Roman Catholics of Lower Canada remain inert,
while the whole continent round them is in a ferment with
Protestant activity and enterprise."[12]

That was written about a century ago, but the only change
required to bring the statement up to date is to make the
opening phrase read, "During the last *four* centuries." Whatever social revival any of the countries mentioned has known
has been the measure of their liberation from the hierarchical
yoke, or the impact of surrounding Protestantism.

After centuries of complete control in the great southern
portion of the American continent, Rome has little to boast
of in the social conditions that obtain there. In the March,
1943, issue of the magazine "Life," the social conditions of the
island of Puerto Rico are represented. Poverty, filth, illiteracy,
high infant mortality, low life expectancy, are the features
marked, over against a little vast wealth and luxury. One
sentence is striking, "Only the health-giving powers of the
salt air and the sun, keep the native children from dropping

---

12. Thomas Babington Macaulay, *History of England,* Twentieth Century Edition, Vol. I, p. 54.

off like flies in their miserable disease-infested pestholes."
One can scarcely imagine that Uncle Sam, so boundless in his
generosity to foreign nations, would leave one of his own
children huddling in such wretchedness. The answer is found
in the further statement: "In Puerto Rico . . . the Roman
Catholic Church is as indigenous to the scene as the court-
house square in the average U. S. county seat; Puerto Ricans
are born into the Catholic faith and die in it as a matter of
course." There seems to be little lifting power in the Roman
system.

Southern Ireland has always been the most backward part
of the British Isles. The tyrant John Bull is, of course, blamed
for that. The English government, one would think, had stud-
ied to oppress poor Ireland. As a matter of fact, the Roman
clergy of Ireland have consistently resisted British attempts to
improve the Irish lot. Claiming that the prerogative of teaching belongs solely to the church, they have refused govern-
mental projects for free education, with the result that Irish
education has lagged far behind Scottish and English
education.

"Life" magazine of October 19, 1942, carried a feature article which was so damaging to the Roman hierarchy of Quebec
Province in Canada that it created a furore. The present writer
lived long enough in Quebec to know that that article was
"more truth than poetry." A people capable of high culture
has long been isolated and retarded in that French Roman
Catholic province. In one of its monographs analyzing the
census of 1931 the Canadian Government reported that illiteracy among French Canadian Catholics over ten years of

age was 6.18 per cent, as against 0.88 per cent among the British races of Canada.[13]

Romanism is essentially anti-democratic and is the foe of our democratic institutions, including our free and compulsory education. Catholic literature intended for Protestant consumption does not show the true Roman hand, but it is not difficult to discover the real temper of the papal system. *America,* a Jesuit magazine, carried the following in its October 31, 1931, issue: "This business of teaching every child indiscriminately how to read and write results in nothing more than mass illiteracy. The man who reads and writes badly, as the great majority do today, is more illiterate than the man who does not read at all. . . This indiscriminate 'education' applied to all alike under State systems is the result of *the heresy of the equality of man.*"[14] Statements like this last give us a hint of a philosophy back of the social suppression of the Roman masses, and help to explain why the papacy and Fascism mix so well. Gladstone, who so courageously championed the religious freedom of Roman Catholics in England, nevertheless referred to Rome's philosophy as "the covetous, domineering, implacable policy represented in the term ultramontanism; the winding up higher and higher, tighter and tighter, of the hierarchical spirit, in total disregard of those elements by which it ought to be checked and balanced; and an unceasing, covert, smouldering war against human freedom, even in its most modest and retiring forms of private life and individual conscience."[15]

Whenever the charge of persecution is laid against Rome,

---

13. Illiteracy and School Attendance, Census Monograph No. 5.
14. Quoted in *The Converted Catholic Magazine,* October, 1944. (Italics ours).
15. *Life of Gladstone,* Vol. I, p. 300.

she puts on an air of offended innocence. Cardinal Gibbons, in his defense of Romanism, completely absolves his church of all guilt and ranges himself and all the Roman clergy on the side of religious freedom! He says:

"In raising my voice against coercion for conscience' sake I am expressing not only my own sentiments, but those of every Catholic priest and layman in the land.

"Our Catholic ancestors, for the last three hundred years, have suffered so much for freedom of conscience that they would rise up in judgment against us were we to become the advocates and defenders of religious persecution. We would be a disgrace to our sires were we to trample on the principle of liberty which they held dearer than life.

"When I denounce the cruelties of the Inquisition I am not standing aloof from the Church, but I am treading in her footprints. . . In all my readings I have yet to find one decree of hers advocating torture or death for conscience' sake. She is indeed intolerant of error; but her only weapons against error are those pointed out by St. Paul to Timothy: 'Preach the word; be instant in season, out of season; reprove, entreat; rebuke with all patience and doctrine.' "[16]

If this were a true representation of the Roman Catholic Church, history would not be the tragic tale of rivers of blood shed in the heat of wars stirred up by the papacy, or spilled in the cold, calculating cruelty of inquisitions sponsored by Rome and her devoted champions.

According to the Roman Catholic historian, Joseph McSorley, it was the Third Council of the Lateran that decreed in 1179 that force should be used against the Albigenses,

---

16. *Faith of our Fathers*, p. 248.

since they would not yield to the preaching of St. Bernard.[17] It was Pope Lucius III who established the inquisitorial method of handing heretics over to the civil powers for "suitable punishment."[18]

In the thirteenth century, when the papacy was enjoying its most undisturbed supremacy, Innocent III trained his guns against the Albigenses, and when repressive measures did not succeed, retaliated for the death of his persecuting legate by calling for a crusade of extermination. The Council of Toulouse, in 1229, commissioned the Inquisition to check further spread of the heresy. In 1233 the Dominicans took over the task, with such success that by the end of the century "the Albigenses had been almost completely eliminated."[19]

Here is a quotation from the same authority: "As heretics became more aggressive, the authorities resorted to more drastic punishment. The ecclesiastical procedure was adjusted to the civil law; and it came to be understood that persons convicted of heresy in Church courts should, as a matter of course, be delivered to the secular power for burning—a procedure devised to free the ecclesiastics of direct responsibility."[20] Some Romanists are ingenuous enough to tell the truth! This historian states further: "In 1233 Gregory IX instituted the Papal Inquisition and placed it in the hands of the Dominicans and the Franciscans, instructing them to co-operate with the local authorities. In its work of suppressing heresy, the Papal Inquisition followed the common procedure of the contemporary courts, accepting anonymous accusations, employing torture to

17. Joseph McSorley, *An Outline History of the Church by Centuries* (St. Louis, Mo., B. Herder Book Co.), Third Edition, 1944, p. 358.
18. Ibid., p. 360.
19. Ibid., p. 411.
20. Ibid., p. 412.

secure confessions, inflicting cruel punishments on convicted persons."[21]

Four popes of the Fourteenth Century are named who united preachings and prisons in their efforts to suppress the Waldenses — John XXII, Benedict XII, Gregory XI, and Clement VII. Despite the papal prisons, the Waldenses were still flourishing a century later.[22]

It was Pope Clement V who put the inquisitorial instrument into the hands of King Philip IV of France, with which he inflicted the horrors of torture and destruction on the Knights Templars.[23]

It was the Council of Constance (1414-1418) which condemned John Huss to be burned at the stake. It was Pope Innocent VIII who "co-operated" with the sixteen year old king of France (Charles VIII, not yet reigning in his own right) in a "crusade" which almost did for the Waldenses what Innocent III had done to the Albigenses.

Knowing right well what a terrible instrument the Inquisition was, Pope Sixtus IV gave it into the hands of Ferdinand and Isabella of Spain in 1476, thus opening a reign of terror at which the world still shudders.

One crime of which Cardinal Gibbons and other Roman apologists are most eager to clear their church is the dastardly massacre of St. Bartholomew, which the Cardinal himself terms an "inhuman slaughter" and an "atrocious butchery," perpetrated against the Huguenots of Paris, August 23, 1572. Quite a story has been "cooked up," laying the entire responsibility on Catherine de Medici. Poulet, the French Catholic historian, leaves all mention of the massacre out of his main

21. *Outline History of the Church by Centuries*, p. 413.
22. Ibid., p. 460.
23. Ibid., p. 462

text, but under "Texts and Documents" at the end of the chapter quotes the Roman version as given by N. A. Weber in *The Christian Era*.[24]

However, in the midst of all this whitewashing of the "atrocious butchery," an outstanding Roman Catholic authority rises up to plead for plain historical honesty. Lord Acton tears away the mask of fiction, admitting that to save Rome's face "a swarm of alleged facts were invented to meet the difficulty." He affirms that two years before the event it was being planned by the most Christian (!) king of France and the queen-mother, who delighted the general of the Franciscans, Mendoça, by their zeal. This high ecclesiastic declared that the king himself had taken part in the massacre. Lord Acton mercilessly reveals that it was with full knowledge of the event, not the garbled account affirmed by other modern Romanists, that the Pope celebrated a Te Deum, instituted a mass of thanksgiving, proclaimed a jubilee, struck a medal, and called Vasari from Florence to memorialize the massacre with paintings on the wall of the hall of kings at the entrance to the Sistine Chapel. The bull proclaiming the jubilee stated quite frankly that it was because "God had armed the king of France *to inflict vengeance on the heretics for the injuries done to religion.*" The political aspect of the horror was quite secondary to the pope.[25]

No! Cardinal Gibbons' offended innocence can never absolve the Roman church, its popes and its councils, from the stains of the richest martyr blood that ever flowed from hu-

24. Dom Charles Poulet, *A History of the Catholic Church* (St. Louis, Mo., B. Herder Book Co., 1939), translated by Raemers, Vol. II, p. 116.
25. Lord Action, *The History of Freedom, and other Essays* (London McMillan and Co., Ltd., 1907).

man veins—rivers and oceans of it. How could this "prince
of the church" declare that he had never found one decree of
the Church of Rome "advocating torture or death for conscience' sake" when the Canon Law gives as the order for
purging heresy: (1) Excommunication, (2) Proscription from
ecclesiastical or civil office, (3) Confiscation of goods, (4)
Death, by sword or fire?[26]   Perhaps he considers that we of
the Protestant heresy have no conscience!

I have refrained from any appeal to the works of Protestant or even neutral historians in regard to the persecutions
of Rome. I am content to let the "bloody harlot" condemn
herself out of her own mouth, by historical admissions that
her popes, councils, and minions have conspired together to
extirpate all who would not bow to her yoke.

John Milton expressed the horror of England at the
slaughter of the Waldenses in the valley of Lucerna, but his
words may well be used to cover the long, dark story of
Rome's persecution of the saints of the Most High.

Avenge, O Lord, thy slaughter'd saints, whose bones
   Lie scatter'd on the Alpine mountains cold;
   Even them who kept thy truth so pure of old,
   When all our fathers worshipp'd stocks and stones,

Forget not: in thy book record their groans
   Who were thy sheep, and in their ancient fold
   Slain by the bloody Piedmontese that roll'd
   Mother with infant down the rocks. Their moans

The vales redoubled to the hills and they
   To heaven. Their martyr'd blood and ashes sow
   O'er all the Italian fields, where still doth sway

---

26. *The Papacy,* p. 136.

The triple tyrant; that from these may grow
   A hundred fold, who, having learn'd thy way,
   Early may fly the Babylonian woe.[27]

Wherever Rome is overshadowed, she whines like a cur, but wherever she is in the ascendency, she roars like a lion and devours like a tiger. If she is curbed today, her nature is not changed. The "principle of liberty" of which Cardinal Gibbons boasts is the principle of liberty for Romanists in a Protestant state, certainly not liberty for Protestants in a Catholic state

In the list of *errors* which he condemned, Pope Pius IX included the following:[28]

"In the present day it is no longer expedient that the Catholic religion should be held as the only religion of the State, to the exclusion of all other forms of worship."[29]

"Hence it has been wisely decided by law, in some Catholic countries, that persons coming to reside therein shall enjoy the public exercise of their own peculiar worship."[30]

Note carefully, this pope is saying that it is an error *not* to give the Roman church exclusive rights in the State, that it is an error to accord any but Roman Catholics freedom of public worship! That is Rome's "principle of liberty." What happened to religious freedom when Spain's democracy fell before Franco's Roman Fascist counter-revolution? It disappeared!

After dyeing her hands in Protestant blood until the sword was wrested from her wreaking grasp, Rome will tell her ignorant devotees of the luxury and cowardice and weakness

---

27. *The Poetical Works of John Milton.*
28. The Syllabus of Pius IX, pp. 77, 78.
29. Allocution "Nemo Vestrum," July 26, 1855.
30. Allocution "Acerbissimus," September 27, 1852.

of Protestants compared with the glorious heroism of Catholic missionaries! Here is a rare bit translated from a French parish bulletin in Quebec:

"Protestantism is not, like the Greek schism, devoid of all proselytism; it writes, it prints, it spreads its books profusely. It even sends missionaries, not indeed wherever there is blood to be spilt; but just as far as its consuls can reach it with his Britannic Majesty's protection does Protestantism hazard its people. . . The Protestant religion does not count martyrs among its apostles. It does not go as far as the witness of blood."

Thanks to Rome, Protestant Christianity numbers its martyrs by the millions!

Chapter Nine

LESSONS FROM ROME

"And why call ye me, Lord, Lord, and do not the things which I say?" *Luke* 6:46.

FOR all her departure from primitive purity and simplicity in doctrine and practice, Rome can nevertheless be our teacher in some matters of grave importance. Modern Protestantism might well examine wherein Rome's continued strength lies, and apply some principles.

The Roman church stands fundamentally for the recognition of authority. The papacy put up a long, hard fight to establish its primacy, but no one now questions papal authority within the vast reaches of the Roman church. The authority of "the church" is an ultimate for all Catholics. Her dogmas are unquestioned by the faithful, on pain of anathemas. The one sin which the Roman church will not brook is the questioning or challenging of her authority.

Now we repudiate the authoritarian system of Rome. We believe in the freedom of the soul and the right of the individual to approach God and know God for himself. We glory in the "liberty wherewith Christ has made us free," the "glorious liberty of the children of God."

But as Rome looks at Protestantism, this liberty of ours is nothing other than a repudiation of all authority. Protestantism, in Rome's eyes, is represented by Dr. Harry Emerson Fosdick and the Federal Council of Churches of Jesus Christ in America. Rome answers our charge of burning Bibles with a counter-charge that we mutilate the Bible, reject its authority, and carve it up to suit our tastes and fancies. The very title of Dr. Fosdick's book, "The Modern Use of the Bible," is suggestive of that attitude of superiority which the modern mind assumes to the Word of God, and which Rome points to as the alternative to her own doctrine of authority. The reformers regarded the Holy Scriptures as the sole rule of faith and practice, and the sons of the reformers throw that sole rule out of the window, torn to shreds by the deft, impious hands of the critic.

With the Bible goes the God of the Bible, and when we charge Rome with a literal idolatry for her veneration of images, relics, and so forth, she comes back with an accusation of intellectual idolatry, in that Protestantism, having rejected the God of revelation, has created a new god, the product of apostate thinking.

Rome is not afraid of modernism. It is her fruitful fishing-pool. Because the human heart cannot be satisfied with the vague, vaporous uncertainties of modernism, Rome addresses herself to those who are under the influence of that emasculated brand of Protestantism, and offers the "authority of the church founded by Jesus Christ" in place of the bewildering uncertainties of indifferentism. Who are they who are making the trek to Rome? Are they those who have been taught in the Scriptures as the Word of God, who have known the Lord Jesus Christ as the very Son of God and their own Saviour from sin, who have nourished their souls on the great and precious promises, who have been accustomed to come with boldness unto the Throne of Grace by the new and living way of Christ crucified, risen, and ascended? We do not find these making the "pilgrimage" to Rome. But I do not wonder at men and women turning away dissatisfied from the empty trough of modernism to what seems to offer a haven of certainty in the authority of the Roman church. My wonder is that the number is not vastly greater. If I had made my recent study of the Roman church as a modernist, ignorant of the blessed certainties of the gospel, I verily believe I should now be on the way to the Roman fold.

All that has to do with modernism. What about our evangelicalism? We profess the supreme authority of God and of His Word: but how does it work out in our lives? It is not only possible, but all too common, to be evangelical in doctrine and modernist in practice, giving mental assent to the great doctrinal tenets of the "faith once for all delivered to the saints," and at the same time refusing obedience to the standards of gospel living enunciated with equal authority in Holy Writ. It is one thing to study the Scriptures for theological exactness, another to submit to them for the regulating of one's life. Dogmatically we acknowledge Christ Jesus as Lord, which title we hold as the title of His deity: then how can we yield other than practical submission to Him as "Lord of our lives and God of our salvation"? Full consecration and complete obedience are the only logical answer to our profession as evangelicals. Rome points to the modernist brand of Protestantism as a fine example of that Scripture which says: "In those days there was no king in Israel: every man did that which was right in his own eyes" (Judg. 21:25). It is ours to demonstrate that there *is* a King in Israel.

Rome has something to teach us in the matter of the training of children. While Protestantism as a whole is making a frantic effort to counteract in one hour each Sunday the effects of the influences of the rest of the week, Rome has its program to sustain consistent pressure of religious teaching on its children every day of every week of every month of every year. The average Protestant home offers no religious training. The average Christian home offers but little. The homes where thanks to God is offered at the table are comparatively few; the homes where family worship is an established institution fewer yet; and the homes where planned, prayerful Christian instruction is regularly given to the children are rare. Whatever the reasons, whether the hectic speed of modern life, the want of training on the part of parents, or a lack of vision and consecration, the fact remains that only in rare instances is home Christian instruction more than a mere modicum.

The case of the school is even less promising. Granted that school-teachers as a class are of a superior grade morally and intellectually, they are probably no more Christian, in the evangelical sense, than other categories. The percentage of enlightened Christians, able to witness a good confession, is certainly not high. Those who are such have indeed a positive influence within the limited sphere in which it may be felt, but they are part of an educational system which is frankly non-Christian. Not only is Christian instruction not allowed in the public school system, on the principle of the separation of church and state, but the philosophies which have dominated the educational field for many years are utterly secularistic, humanistic, and mechanistic, as Dr. Robert L. Cooke has unanswerably shown in his work, "Philosophy, Education and Certainty." That creates an atmosphere which is poisonous to the soul of our youth, an atmosphere which a real Christian teacher may be strong enough to neutralize, but which few of our children can escape for long in the course of their schooling. Where there are no checks to the expression of the philosophies in question, in the form of Christian teachers, one does not wonder at the increase in lawlessness and the spectacle of religious scorners, full-blown infidels, in the early years of high school.

To sum up, we know that our children do not receive Christian instruction in the public school—we would not want them to unless it were under believing instructors. Moreover, there is a philosophic basis to modern education which throws around it an atmosphere not conducive to spiritual culture. Our children spend much of their time, both at and after school, with children from non-Christian homes and in a purely secular atmosphere. As I have already indicated, only in the rare instances is a serious effort made in the home to build up around the child a strong support of Christian instruction and training. It is therefore left to the church to do two things—supply the lack of home training and counteract the subtle effect of exposure to secularism the whole week. How do we go about it? Sunday school, Christian Endeavor, and Young People's Club are our specific, so far as organization is concerned, in addition to the public worship in which all are expected to join. Thus a well-organized Protestant church devotes three hours per week to specialized training of the young. One of these hours is partly social, with devotions and some exhortation, one hour is expressional, and part of the other is instructional. For those who do not come from vital Christian homes, here is the average good church's offer: three hours under direct Christian influence, with one-half to three quarters of an hour only of definite instruction in the elements of the Christian faith. It is hopelessly inadequate.

Rome can teach us here. She knows that religious training at home can be relied upon only in rare instances, and she certainly knows that secular education will not make good Catholics. So, while buttressing home training by every means available, she plans to have the child under her immediate and direct influence as soon and as long as she can. The separate school is the answer. The church educates the child, not only giving stated periods each day for religious instruction and exercises, but putting religion at the basis of all the instruction given. There is no disharmony between what the child learns in the catechism and what he learns in his zoology class. It is all of a piece. The child is taught that his whole life revolves around the church as the mighty hub.

Say what we will against the Roman dogmas as contrary to Scriptures: say what we will about the tyranny of the system: we must admit that Rome is diligent in the care of her children, and we could well take a leaf out of her book in the care of ours. Rome makes it a matter of obligation on her people to send their children to the Catholic school. Thus while Protestant churches bemoan the fatal leak, Rome stops it. I am persuaded that we shall not be fulfilling our task in regard to our youth until we have them under positive Christian influence and teaching seven days a week. The situation becomes more imperative as lawlessness increases. I know that after all we can do, it is only the Holy Spirit who can make Christians, but He works through the consecrated efforts of the people of God.

The sanctity of marriage is another subject in which the Roman church can be the teacher of Protestantism. Between

20 and 25 per cent of American marriages end in divorce, and the trend is an increase. We know, of course, that the bulk of these divorces take place among those who are no more Protestant than Catholic, and are certainly not Christian. But in the circle of nominal Protestant Christianity there has been a fearful lowering of the standards. In all too many cases Bible standards have been forgotten and world standards adopted or at least tolerated, till a pastor would dare to refuse Christian marriage to divorced people only if he were prepared to read his resignation the following Sunday. Even in

When Roman Catholics are preparing for marriage, they do some circles claiming the title "fundamental" there is a looseness in this matter which amounts to unmitigated scandal. not only visit the county court house to receive a license, but they wait upon the priest, individually. Each one is instructed emphatically in the sanctity of the marriage bond, and signs, as under oath, his or her intention to contract a life-partnership dissoluble only by death. One who enters Roman Catholic marriage with the idea of getting a divorce if it does not work out perjures himself, besides committing the sin of desecrating a sacrament. He clearly understands what it is all about. If divorce is sought, it constitutes a breach of oath, and is not recognized by the church. Remarriage while the former partner lives is forbidden. If Catholics go ahead and so remarry before the civil authority, it is a mortal sin; if they go to a Protestant minister, it is an act of apostasy, punishable with excommunication.

When Protestants marry, they obtain their license and go to the minister. If the service is discussed at all, it is usually to discover what form will please the bride. The "till death do us part" formula is one of the pretty sentiments of the service, in too many cases conveying little impression of the solemn obligations and the high sanctity of the new relationship. Few Protestants could tell you the day after the marriage to what they committed themselves, if to anything. Divorce becomes the recognized escape from the common difficulties of the wedded state, and a conscienceless society accepts "repeats" as normal, the churches too often falling in line to avoid offense. Protestantism needs to get back its voice and shout from the housetops the shame of the breakdown of the holy bond. If we claim to be in any sense the church of Jesus Christ, it is time to act according to His teachings, which declare unequivocally: "Whosoever shall put away his wife, except it be for fornication, and shall marry another, committeth adultery: and whoso marrieth her which is put away doth commit adultery" (Matt. 19:9).

The "mixed marriage" is also a matter in which we might learn something from Rome. The teaching of Scripture is clear enough on this question. "Be ye not unequally yoked together with unbelievers: for what fellowship hath righteousness with unrighteousness? and what communion hath light with darkness? And what concord hath Christ with Belial? or what part hath he that believeth with an infidel? And what agreement hath the temple of God with idols? for ye are the temple of the living God" (II Cor. 6:14-16). It is true that these words are not confined to the marital relation, but if they do not apply here, in the closest of human bonds, they apply nowhere.

The reasons for such an injunction are not far to seek. Every observant Christian must have seen the breakdown in Christian profession on the part of great numbers who have married in defiance of this command to marry "only in the

Lord" (I Cor. 7:39), and the struggle and heartache of those who have tried to live for Christ after entering such an unequal union. A home so constituted can never be a truly Christian home, and the handicap laid on one who seeks to train children in the Christian way is in such a case almost insuperable. The results in the vast majority of cases do not justify the experiment. In the case of one of the parties being brought to the Lord after marriage, special grace may be expected, but where the marriage is contracted in disobedience, it will require much repentance and much travail to overcome the wilfully assumed hindrance.

We can only be thankful for churches where this teaching is given the young people, but such churches are all too few, and all too few the ministers who will reinforce the teaching with a refusal to officiate at the union of a believer with an unbeliever. How many churches would stand back of their minister in such a refusal, in the case, say, of the leading elder's daughter marrying an unconverted man? Where can church discipline be found that would take care of such affairs?

Now Rome's attitude on this question of mixed marriages irks most Protestants, but my only criticism is that she is more tolerant of mixed marriages than she professes to be. When Rome speaks of a "mixed marriage," she does not, of course, mean the union of an evangelical believer with an unconverted person, but the marriage of a Catholic with a non-Catholic. We must remember that according to the Roman teaching the Roman church is the church founded by Christ, and true religion dwells with her alone. Therefore, it is a matter of salvation to remain in communion with the Catholic church. Seeing, then, the danger of her children drifting from her by their association with non-Catholics, and the still greater danger of the offspring of such marriage being lost to her, the Roman church first of all forbids mixed marriages, and then grants dispensations on certain rigid conditions. Now ideally she ought not to grant dispensations at all, but knowing right well that many Catholics would go off to a magistrate or a Protestant minister rather than be denied the desired partner (thus committing a mortal sin or, still worse, an act of apostasy), she "wisely" yields to the weaknesses of her children and tightens her hold upon them and their offspring, hoping in the meantime to win the non-Catholic spouse.

Four privileges are withheld in the case of a mixed marriage: the service may not be held in the church, the banns are not read, and the blessing of the ring and the nuptial blessing are omitted from the ceremony. By these means the appearance of disapproval at least is upheld.

But before the dispensation is granted both parties are required to sign certain solemn promises, which are in the form of an oath for the non-Catholic party. Here are the statements:

Agreement and Promises to Be Signed by the Catholic Party

"I, the undersigned, a member of the Catholic Church, wishing to contract marriage with the non-Catholic party whose signature is affixed above to this mutual agreement, being of sound mind and perfectly free, and only after understanding fully the import of my action, do hereby enter into this mutual agreement, understanding that the execution of this agreement and the promises therein contained are made in contemplation of and in consideration for the consent, marriage, and consequent change of my status, and I, therefore, hereby agree:

(1) That I shall have all my children, both boys and girls, that may be born of this union, baptized and educated solely in the faith of the Roman Catholic Church. I understand that in case of my death, or in the event of a dispute, the custody of all the children shall be given to such guardians as to assure the faithful execution of this covenant and promise;

(2) That I will practice my Catholic religion faithfully, and will strive, especially by example, prayer and the frequentation of the Sacraments, to bring about the conversion of my consort;

(3) That I will lead a married life in conformity with the teaching of the Catholic Church regarding birth control, realizing fully the attitude of the Catholic Church in this regard;

(4) That no other marriage ceremony shall take place before or after this ceremony by the Catholic priest."

Agreement and Promises to Be Signed by the Non-Catholic Party

"I, the undersigned, not a member of the Catholic Church, wishing to contract marriage with the Catholic party whose signature is also hereinafter affixed to this mutual agreement, being of sound mind and perfectly free, and only after understanding fully the import of my action, do hereby enter into this mutual agreement, understanding that the execution of this agreement and the promises therein contained are made in contemplation of and in consideration for the consent, marriage and consequent change of status of the hereinafter mentioned Catholic party, and I, therefore, hereby agree:

(1) That I will not interfere in the least with the free exercise of the Catholic party's religion;

(2) That I will adhere to the doctrine of the sacred in-

dissolubility of the marriage bond, so that I cannot contract a second marriage while my consort is still alive, even though a civil divorce may have been obtained;

(3) That all the children, both boys and girls, that may be born of this union shall be baptized and educated solely in the faith of the Roman Catholic Church, even in the event of the death of my Catholic consort. In case of dispute, I, furthermore, hereby fully agree that the custody of all the children shall be given to such guardians as to assure the faithful execution of this covenant and promise, in the event that I cannot fulfill it myself;

(4) That I will lead a married life in conformity with the teaching of the Catholic Church regarding birth control, realizing fully the attitude of the Catholic Church in this regard;

(5) That no other marriage ceremony shall take place before or after this ceremony by the Catholic priest.

In testimony of which agreement, I do hereby solemnly swear that I will observe the above agreement and faithfully execute the promises therein contained, and do now affix my signature in approval thereof."

Whatever we may think of this one-sided arrangement, we must admit that from the Roman point of view, it is the most consistent, and indeed the only possible attitude, if dispensations for mixed marriages are to be granted at all. The tragedy is that so many who call themselves Protestants, but who are simply non-Catholics, enter into such a contract with little or no concern. Dr. O'Brien says: "The fact that the vast majority of non-Catholics experience little or no religious scruple in signing the required promises testifies to the levity with which denominational ties rest upon them."[1] That such a statement can be published without fear of challenge constitutes Rome's justification for her belief that Protestantism is a dead issue, no more to be feared. This surely is a call to our churches to ring out in clarion notes the faith which the Reformation restored, over against the accumulation of "damnable heresies" which are imposed on the dupes of Rome. In face, too, of Rome's seizure of generations yet unborn, a solemn responsibility rests on us of the evangelical faith to safeguard our children and our children's children by the establishment of truly Christian homes, undivided and uncompromising in their testimony.

---

1. O'Brien, *The Faith of Millions,* p. 332.

BIBLIOGRAPHY

The bibliography on this subject is almost limitless. Only those are listed here which are mentioned in the text.

The Faith of Millions, John A. O'Brien, Ph.D.,
  Our Sunday Visitor, Huntington, Ind., 1938.

The Papacy, Dr. J. A. Wylie,
  Hamilton, Adams and Co., London, 1867.

The Sacrifice of Christ, R. W. Grace,
  J. F. Wagner, New York, 1937.

The Catholic Church from Within,
  Longmans, Green, and Co., London, 1901.

The Faith of our Fathers, Cardinal Gibbons,
  P. J. Kenedy, New York, 110th Edition.

The Catholic Catechism, Cardinal Gasparri,
  (Authorized Translation by Hugh Pope, O.P.)
  P. J. Kenedy & Sons, New York, Third Printing.

The Life of Alexander Whyte, G. F. Barbour,
  George H. Doran, New York, 1925.

Our Priceless Heritage, Dr. Henry M. Woods,
  The Evangelical Press, Harrisburg, Pa., 1941.

Eternal Priesthood, Cardinal Manning,
  Burns and Oates, London, 1883.

Mariology, Pohle-Preuss,
  B. Herder Book Co., St. Louis, Mo., 1914.

The Life of the Blessed Virgin Mary, Mary of
  Jesus of Agreda (abridged by De Caesare)
  Translated by Abbé Joseph A. Boullan,
  P. J. Kenedy & Sons, New York.

Catechism of the Council of Trent for Parish Priests,
  (Translated by McHugh and Callan)
  Second Revised Edition, 1937,
  Joseph F. Wagner, New York.

Life of Gladstone, Morley,
  Edward Floyd, London, 1908.

John Hus, Benito Mussolini,
  (Translated by Clifford Parker)
  Zondervan, Grand Rapids, 1929.

Inside Europe, John Gunther,
  Harper & Bros., New York, 1938.

History of England, Thomas Babington Macaulay,
  Twentieth Century Edition.

An Outline History of the Church by Centuries, Joseph McSorley,
  B. Herder Book Co., St. Louis, Mo., 1944.

A History of the Catholic Church, Dom Charles Poulet,
  B. Herder Book Co., St. Louis, Mo., 1939.

The History of Freedom and Other Essays,
  McMillan & Co., London, 1907.

The Little Flower Prayer Book,
  Carmelite Press, Chicago, 4th Edition.

Truth vs. Dogma

J. C. Macaulay

In this scholarly work Mr. Macaulay explains clearly and fairly the real differences between the faith of Roman Catholics and that of Protestant Christians. He presents the position of the Roman Church with accuracy, quoting from standard authorities in analyzing its major doctrines.

The purpose of the book is twofold: to point out the freedom of the gospel of Jesus Christ to those who may have been confused by the tenets and rites of Rome, and to inform Protestant believers.

These absorbing messages were originally delivered by the author to his congregation in the Wheaton (Ill.) Bible Church.

About the Author

Born of Scottish parents in Belfast, Ireland, Mr. J. C. Macaulay was converted at the age of nine and received his education in Scotland with training in Glasgow University.

Soon after Mr. Macaulay emigrated to Canada in 1920, he was ordained to the gospel ministry in Dufferin Street Baptist Church, Toronto, and in 1925 married Miss Helen Edna Duncombe. His ministry has extended to Bible Conferences including Erieside, Ben Lippen, and Canadian Keswick of which he was once a director. He has held pastorates in Cleveland, Ohio; Quebec City and Sault Ste. Marie, Ontario and since 1939 has been pastor of the Wheaton Bible Church.

Mr. Macaulay is the author of two volumes of devotional exposition in St. John's Gospel —"The Word Made Flesh," and "Obedient Unto Death."